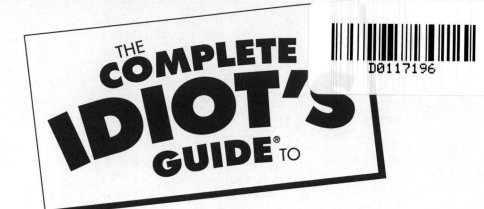

THE
COMPLETE
IDIOT'S
GUIDE® TO

Ultimate Fighting®

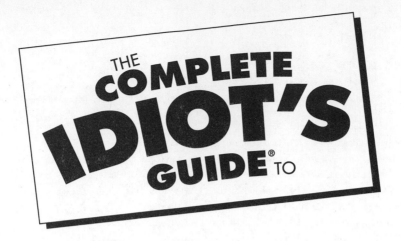

THE
COMPLETE IDIOT'S GUIDE® TO

Ultimate Fighting®

by Rich "Ace" Franklin and Jon F. Merz

ALPHA

A member of Penguin Group (USA) Inc.

ALPHA BOOKS

Published by the Penguin Group

Penguin Group (USA) Inc., 375 Hudson Street, New York, New York 10014, USA

Penguin Group (Canada), 90 Eglinton Avenue East, Suite 700, Toronto, Ontario M4P 2Y3, Canada (a division of Pearson Penguin Canada Inc.)

Penguin Books Ltd., 80 Strand, London WC2R 0RL, England

Penguin Ireland, 25 St. Stephen's Green, Dublin 2, Ireland (a division of Penguin Books Ltd.)

Penguin Group (Australia), 250 Camberwell Road, Camberwell, Victoria 3124, Australia (a division of Pearson Australia Group Pty. Ltd.)

Penguin Books India Pvt. Ltd., 11 Community Centre, Panchsheel Park, New Delhi—110 017, India

Penguin Group (NZ), 67 Apollo Drive, Rosedale, North Shore, Auckland 1311, New Zealand (a division of Pearson New Zealand Ltd.)

Penguin Books (South Africa) (Pty.) Ltd., 24 Sturdee Avenue, Rosebank, Johannesburg 2196, South Africa

Penguin Books Ltd., Registered Offices: 80 Strand, London WC2R 0RL, England

International Standard Book Number: 978-1-59257-655-5
Library of Congress Catalog Card Number: 2007922828

09 08   8 7 6 5 4 3

Interpretation of the printing code: The rightmost number of the first series of numbers is the year of the book's printing; the rightmost number of the second series of numbers is the number of the book's printing. For example, a printing code of 07-1 shows that the first printing occurred in 2007.

Printed in the United States of America

Note: This publication contains the opinions and ideas of its authors. It is intended to provide helpful and informative material on the subject matter covered. It is sold with the understanding that the authors and publisher are not engaged in rendering professional services in the book. If the reader requires personal assistance or advice, a competent professional should be consulted.

The authors and publisher specifically disclaim any responsibility for any liability, loss, or risk, personal or otherwise, which is incurred as a consequence, directly or indirectly, of the use and application of any of the contents of this book.

Most Alpha books are available at special quantity discounts for bulk purchases for sales promotions, premiums, fund-raising, or educational use. Special books, or book excerpts, can also be created to fit specific needs.

For details, write: Special Markets, Alpha Books, 375 Hudson Street, New York, NY 10014.

Publisher: *Marie Butler-Knight*
Editorial Director/Acquiring Editor: *Mike Sanders*
Managing Editor: *Billy Fields*
Development Editor: *Ginny Bess Munroe*
Senior Production Editor: *Janette Lynn*
Copy Editor: *Jeff Rose*

Cover Designer: *Bill Thomas*
Book Designer: *Trina Wurst*
Indexer: *Angie Bess*
Layout: *Chad Dressler*
Proofreader: *John Etchison*

Contents at a Glance

Contents

Foreword

I was always a boxing guy. I grew up watching the sport on television every week, I fought as an amateur, and even considered turning pro for a while. For me, there was nothing better than a good fight—two guys putting it on the line and settling everything with their fists.

So when the Ultimate Fighting Championship® launched in 1993, I was skeptical, just like most boxing fans. You had 175-pound guys fighting 400-pound guys, there were few rules, and it just didn't seem to have any rhyme or reason to it.

But fast forward a few years, and I ran into John Lewis, a fighter and a Brazilian Jiu-Jitsu Black Belt. He had a bunch of mixed martial artists around his gym, and after working out with these guys for a bit and talking with them, I saw the sport in an entirely new light. Notice I said "sport" and not "spectacle," because it was the spectacle of the early UFC® events that gave mixed martial arts and the fighters a bad name. These weren't barroom brawlers; these were highly skilled, well-trained, intelligent athletes competing in a sport that mixed boxing with jiu-jitsu, judo, kickboxing, and wrestling. Add in the weight classes and unified rules that had been implemented over the years, and I instantly became a fan.

The rest of the world was slow to catch on, though, so, along with my partners Lorenzo and Frank Fertitta, we decided that if we showed everyone just how special these fighters were and how exciting this sport was, it would take off. To do that, we bought what at the time was a dying brand, and we presented this the way it always should have been presented—as a sport.

In the book you're holding in your hands right now, you'll read about the history of Ultimate Fighting® and the UFC, the rules of the sport, and the ups and downs we went through to get here. Even more importantly, you'll read about the fighters who made the UFC what it is today, the intense training it takes to get to the UFC, as well as the techniques necessary to stay there. And what better representative is there to explain the intricacies of this sport than the former middleweight champion of the world, Rich Franklin?

Rich epitomizes what this sport is all about. He's a former high school math teacher with a Master's degree in Education, and he's also one of the best fighters to ever step foot inside the Octagon™. He doesn't need to do this for a living; he does it because he loves the training, the competition, and having the forum to prove himself as the best 185-pound fighter in the world. In fact, most of our athletes are just like Rich, and that's why it's an honor for me to be able to bring them to you on television and in arenas around the world, and why I thank you for picking up this book and supporting the most exciting sport in the world.

Dana White

President, Ultimate Fighting Championship

Introduction

A 30 Foot Octagon™.

Two supremely conditioned athletes.

And three or five rounds to prove themselves better than the other.

Welcome to the Ultimate Fighting Championship® brand of mixed martial arts, or UFC® as it's also known. UFC events represent the most exciting development in combat sports and its matches are among the most popular pay-TV viewing events anywhere in the world.

But what is UFC? How did it evolve from a crude form of fighting to become the powerhouse of mixed martial arts it is today? What are the fighting styles that make up a UFC fighter, and how do the styles mandate certain strategies? And what exactly is going on in the midst of all those flying fists, kicks, throws, takedowns, and submission holds?

We'll guide you through everything UFC—from the beginning of it all to the future of the UFC promotion itself—until you become as well versed in the Ultimate Fighting Championship events as many of the commentators themselves.

What's in This Book

Whether you're a recent convert to the world of UFC fights or a lifelong fan, the UFC is far more than a simple one-dimensional sport where two fighters simply attempt to beat each other up. The UFC has a sense of history and evolution that far surpasses what most people realize. Combined with that is a very scientific approach to understanding the mechanics of fighting, depending on the styles employed, that adds yet another fascinating aspect to the UFC. Put simply, the UFC is part sport, part science, part art, and 100 percent thrills. This book is designed to help you make the most of your own personal UFC experience.

We've divided the book into five distinct parts.

In **Part 1, "The World of Ultimate Fighting® Events,"** we take you back to the origins of mixed martial arts and how MMA eventually evolved into the Ultimate Fighting Championship. We'll look at the influence of the Gracie family and how the introduction of groundfighting changed the way a lot of people looked at sport combat. We'll also examine how the rules have changed from an "anything goes" perception that led to events being banned, to how a new management team and their work with state athletic commissions helped pave the way for the UFC's rise to superstardom. We'll look at how the current UFC rules help protect the fighter, and how those fighters achieve their victories.

In **Part 2, "Today's Ultimate Fighter™ Athlete,"** we'll meet the new breed of gladiators looking to stake their claim to the UFC's highest levels of success. To do so, they need to be as well versed in as many fighting styles as possible. We'll look at the variety of fighting arts employed by UFC competitors and the strengths and weaknesses inherent to them. Based on the strengths of the styles and the fighters themselves, we'll also examine what strategies the savviest fighters use to enhance their chances of achieving a victory.

Part 3, "'As Real As It Gets'®," takes us right into the Octagon™ arena itself for an up-close and personal look at how the fight unfolds. We'll see how fighters use their timing and footwork to outstrike an opponent. Then we'll knock heads and look at how things get tight in the clinch as each warrior looks to sneak in a knockout or maneuver for the takedown and eventual submission.

In **Part 4, "When the Fight Goes to the Ground,"** we'll get down to business on the mat. As the fighters try to position themselves for a submission or "ground-and-pound" victory, we'll take you inside the action and explain how each position offers its own unique advantages and disadvantages. Whether you're on top in the guard or on the bottom while your opponent has the side mount, you'll know just what each fighter is hoping to achieve as they work against the clock and each other.

Finally, in **Part 5, "What It Takes to Be an Ultimate Fighter™ Athlete,"** we'll show you how top UFC fighter Rich Franklin prepares to do battle with his opponents. We'll look at how Rich sizes up his competition, lays out a game plan, assembles a great team, and then trains to achieve victory. We'll also get an inside look at how Rich keeps himself in superior condition leading up to a fight, and what he does post-fight to help ensure proper recovery and a solid foundation for his next event. Finally, Rich will take us on a very special journey—his own rise to fame as a UFC champion.

Ultimate Extras

To help make this even more fun, we've highlighted lots of tips, facts, and special information throughout the book. Look for the following boxes as you read and enjoy the unique information they have to offer:

> **FIGHTSPEAK**
>
> "Fightspeak" sidebars provide you with definitions of UFC terms and other technical language introduced throughout the book and used in UFC events. By learning these terms, you'll know exactly what UFC commentators and other fans are talking about.

> **FIGHTER FACTS**
>
> "Fighter Facts" provide a sampling of cool trivia relating to the UFC, fighters themselves, and special statistics used by UFC enthusiasts to determine the likely outcome of each fight.

> **Notable Fights**
>
> We'll take a look at some of the most spectacular UFC events in these boxes. We'll highlight 20 of the hardest-hitting most-throwdown-choked-out bouts ever witnessed in the UFC.

Our last sidebar, "Pro-Files," gets you up-close and personal with the current crop of UFC gladiators who are already champions or looking to win a title. We'll look at four from each weight class—fighters whose names you need to remember.

PRO-FILES — *Rich "Ace" Franklin*

(Photo courtesy Zuffa, LLC)

Fighting out of: Cincinnati, Ohio
Date of Birth: October 5, 1974
Height: 6' 1"
Weight: 185 lbs.
Weightclass: Middleweight
Former UFC Middleweight Champion

Known for his excellent striking skills, condition, and being well rounded in his techniques, Rich typically trains for at least five hours every day, regardless of who his opponent is. Notable fights include a first-round technical knockout win against Ken Shamrock and a five-round unanimous decision win over David Louiseau. A four-year veteran of mixed martial arts, Rich was a high school teacher before becoming a full-time UFC competitor. He holds a Bachelor's degree in Mathematics and a Master's degree in Education from the University of Cincinnati.

UFC LEGENDS

Similar to our "Pro-Files" sidebar, "UFC Legends" will spotlight the top names that helped the UFC evolve into the powerhouse it is today. Veterans of spectacular fights, these retired professionals have since gone on to the UFC Hall of Fame or to coach the new generation of UFC greats.

Acknowledgments

A book like this doesn't spring onto the shelves overnight, and we would like to thank a few people for their help along the way. Our editor Mike Sanders deserves heaps of praise for his vision, guidance, and never-ending enthusiasm for the work itself.

First and foremost, I would like to thank God for watching me through life. I'd like to say thanks to my family: my mother and father, my wife Beth, and my brother Greg for supporting me. I'd like to say thanks to my trainers Jorge, Neal, Rob, Mike, and Doc Youtsler. Without them, I couldn't have attained the title. Thanks to my friends Steve, Shawn, and Josh Rafferty, and Kerry Schall. These guys were with me in the beginning. I'll never forget the days of training in the shed. I'd like to thank the men behind the scenes: my manager Monte Cox, the guys at American Fighter, Jeff Adler & JT Stewart. And finally, I'd like to thank the UFC for the opportunities that I've had in life.

Jon would like to thank Mark Davis, Masaaki Hatsumi, Stephen K. Hayes, Ken Savage, Paul Etherington, and "anyone else who has ever tried to take my head off or grind my face into the ground." Thanks also to all his friends at the Boston Martial Arts Center—Arthur, Dennis, Zaino, Tim, Curt, Dave, and everyone else. Big thanks to his agent Robert G. (Bob) Diforio for landing this project. And last, but most importantly, a huge thanks to his beautiful wife Joyce and his two sons, Jack and Will, for their love and endless smile—as well as the shock-and-awe of their ambush tackle-and-tickle technique.

Special Thanks to the Ultimate Fighting Championship®

The Complete Idiot's Guide to Ultimate Fighting® would not be possible without the kind assistance and expert oversight of the Ultimate Fighting Championship organization itself and Zuffa, LLC. Their excitement and zeal for this project, as well as their review of the work for its technical and factual accuracy, is most heartily appreciated.

Trademarks

All terms mentioned in this book that are known to be or are suspected of being trademarks or service marks have been appropriately capitalized. Alpha Books and Penguin Group (USA) Inc. cannot attest to the accuracy of this information. Use of a term in this book should not be regarded as affecting the validity of any trademark or service mark.

ULTIMATE FIGHTING®, ULTIMATE FIGHTING CHAMPIONSHIP®, UFC®, The Ultimate Fighter®, AS REAL AS IT GETS® and the eight-sided competition mat are federally registered trademarks and/or service marks of Zuffa, LLC and are used herein solely pursuant to a license granted by Zuffa, LLC. ULTIMATE FIGHTING® and ULTIMATE FIGHTING CHAMPIONSHIP® are proprietary brand names; accordingly, any references herein to such terms refer exclusively to the brand of mixed martial arts events promoted by Zuffa, LLC. The Octagon and Octagon are trademarks and or service marks of Zuffa, LLC.

Part 1

The World of Ultimate Fighting® Events

In this first part, we take a look at the history of the Ultimate Fighting Championship®. From its early days through the so-called "dark ages" to its refined emergence as a legitimate sports powerhouse, we see how the UFC® has embraced change, established rules, and raised the bar for itself. The result is something truly special.

A History of Competition

In This Chapter

- ◆ The Origins of Mixed Martial Arts
- ◆ The First Ultimate Fighting Championship®
- ◆ Crazy for Gracie
- ◆ Few Rules, Few Opportunities
- ◆ Beating Bad Press: The Evolution of the UFC®
- ◆ A "Smashing" Success

People have been fascinated with fights and fighters for thousands of years. From the earliest pugilistic bouts of ancient Greece to the organized matches of wrestling and boxing, spectators enjoy a good fight. Whether it's a vicarious thrill or a genuine appreciation for the talent and raw nerve necessary to pit oneself against another in combat, there's no doubt that fighting always draws a crowd.

While the twentieth century progressed and Hollywood capitalized on the advent of television and pay cable enterprises, boxing and wrestling both enjoyed their heyday as the premier fight-oriented sports platforms.

But that all changed in the early 1990s. A few pioneering spirits brought an entirely new concept to mass audiences: mixed martial arts events that pitted competitors from various martial arts styles against one another in so-called "no holds barred" fights.

In this chapter, we take a look at the origin of mixed martial arts and how it evolved from spectacle to sport and into the powerhouse known as the Ultimate Fighting Championship®.

Origins of Mixed Martial Arts

Dating back to the Thirty-third Olympic Games held in Ancient Greece in 648 B.C.E, the origins of *mixed martial arts* are often the subject of varying perspectives. The Greek art of Pankration, translated as "all power" or "all strength," was perhaps the first combat sport, and over the years there have been other regular occurrences of fighters from differing styles pitting themselves against one another. As the years passed, boxers encountered wrestlers and often put their skills to the test.

Vale Tudo

It wasn't until the popularity of Vale Tudo in Brazil in the early 1930s that mixed martial arts finally found a place to blossom.

> **FIGHTSPEAK**
>
> Some older fans of the sport like to refer to **mixed martial arts** (MMA) as "no holds barred" fighting, but this is incorrect. As MMA evolved, so did the set of rules designed to protect the fighters and help push the sport as a viable platform for fans, investors and businesses. There have always been rules! In fact, they're covered in the next chapter.

Vale Tudo is Portuguese for "anything goes" and refers specifically to the fights that occurred (and which still apparently take place) with a bare minimum of restrictions. Most people refer to Vale Tudo as one part of the foundation that helps make up modern MMA. Others support the notion that Vale Tudo itself can be considered a fighting style.

In the 1960s a Brazilian television program, *Vale Tudo on TV* took the name Vale Tudo and began broadcasting select fights between opposing martial arts styles. Another show, *Heroes of the Ring*, was produced by none other than Hélio Gracie, one of the famed Gracie family (more about the Gracie clan in a moment).

PRO-FILES **Tim "The Maine-iac" Sylvia**

(*Photo courtesy Zuffa, LLC*)

Fighting out of: Davenport, Iowa
Born: 3/5/76
Height: 6'8"
Weight: 265 lbs.
Weight class: Heavyweight
Two-time UFC Heavyweight Champion

Hailing from Maine and now fighting out of Iowa, Tim is a former semi-pro football player turned mixed martial artist who entered the pro ranks in 2001. Known for his devastating right hand, takedown defense, and enormous reach, Sylvia was unbeaten in his first 16 bouts and is only the second man in UFC history to win the heavyweight title twice. He holds victories over noted standouts Andrei Arlovski (twice), Ricco Rodriguez, and Jeff Monson.

Vale Tudo definitely helped pave the way for the future of MMA more than 40 years ago. Without its success in Brazil, there's no way it could have been exported to the rest of the world. Using Brazilian Jiu-Jitsu as the cornerstone of the Vale Tudo events, the stage was also set for the emergence of Brazilian Jiu-Jitsu.

Jiu-Jitsu

Indigenous forms of martial arts were commonplace in many Asian countries. As styles evolved, they inevitably migrated to nearby countries. Japanese Jujutsu evolved as a pragmatic all-encompassing form of martial arts practiced by the warrior elite of Japan—the samurai. Throughout much of Japan's history the country was embroiled in civil war. Samurai needed methods to protect themselves on the battlefield while excelling in their ability to kill their enemy. Jujutsu became their chosen method for doing just that.

By the end of the seventeenth century, many different forms of Jujutsu existed. These "ryuha" placed priority on different areas and their specializations were many and varied.

As power shifted from the Shogun to the Emperor at the end of the Edo period, so, too, did the need for trained warriors. The emperor issued a decree forbidding training in many of these military-oriented arts as a way of hopefully quelling any would-be threats to his power. As a result, many Jujutsu schools stripped the lethal aspects of their training out of their respective curricula. Nowhere was this more evident than when Jigoro Kano created the art of Judo and touted it as superior to the older arts that he had grown up on.

Brazilian Jiu-Jitsu was developed when a Japanese businessman named Mitsuyo Maeda immigrated to Brazil around 1910. Maeda was a recognized Judo and Jujutsu practitioner who had studied at the Kudokan in Tokyo, Japan. When Maeda studied, the Kudokan was in the process of absorbing into its teachings more ground-fighting techniques (Ne-waza) that had been systematized by teachers of the Fusen-ryu Jiu-Jitsu style. Apparently, Fusen-ryu masters had fought Kudokan students and won the matches, leading Kudokan seniors to incorporate select Fusen-ryu techniques into the established Kudokan curriculum.

Maeda traveled extensively through the world, engaging in a variety of fights that pitted his style of fighting against other styles. He would eventually earn the nickname "Count Combat" (Conde Koma) in Spain in 1908, for his extensive abilities to submit a variety of boxers and wrestlers to his technique.

Maeda's immigration to Brazil would probably not have occurred had it not been for Brazilian businessman Gastão Gracie's help. In exchange for helping him secure a consulate post, Maeda offered to teach Gastão's son Carlos Jiu-Jitsu. Carlos would later go on to teach his four brothers this style of Jiu-Jitsu, most notably Hélio Gracie.

Doctors had forbidden the frail Hélio, the youngest member of the Gracie clan, from participating in strenuous exercise. Hélio instead watched the Jiu-Jitsu techniques and memorized all of them by the time he was sixteen years old, eventually becoming the family's most recognizable instructor.

By the latter part of the twentieth century, Hélio had introduced a second generation of Gracies to the wonders of Brazilian Jiu-Jitsu. Thinking outside the box, this second generation aspired to more than simply winning various matches: they wanted to introduce the world to their fighting method.

UFC 1: The Beginning

After settling in the United States in 1978, Rorion Gracie spent years trying to spread the word about his recently trademarked style of martial arts—Gracie Jiu-Jitsu. But he found it tough going even after impressing the likes of martial arts luminary Benny "The Jet" Urquidez.

An article in *Playboy Magazine* in 1989, however, changed his fortune. Los Angeles advertising executive Arthur Davie was impressed enough to eventually explore the art. Along the way, he connected with director John Milius and he, Milius, and Gracie would often discuss martial arts after classes.

After he left the world of advertising in 1991, Davie agreed to help publicize a new videotape series called *Gracies in Action*. Each tape featured challenge matches between the Gracies and other styles. While Davie had a winner on his hands in terms of direct mail sales, he knew the potential existed for something much bigger. He thought it belonged on television.

Davie and Gracie pitched the idea for a televised competition to Milius, who was excited by the concept. Milius researched the concept further, noting that a lack of boxing commissions in many states might help the competition avoid niggling questions about safety. By October of 1992, the three men had a detailed proposal ready to circulate.

But the big Pay-Per-View (PPV) platforms wanted no part of it. PPV hadn't yet found its monetary niche and the big broadcasters weren't confident the show would pull in numbers. Davie found himself with one last choice: Semaphore Entertainment Group (SEG).

Fortunately, Davie found sympathetic ears in SEG and the firm agreed to pour $400,000 into the project. This was further aided by private investments from many of Gracie's students who heard Davie and Gracie pitch them on the concept after they had formed WOW Productions.

Davie and Gracie initially wanted the winner of the first competition to walk away with $110,000 and have a fight card of sixteen combatants. SEG whittled that down to eight and offered a top prize of $50,000 instead.

Fighters from various styles were added to the card—eight in all, representing a wide spectrum of fighting expertise. Minimal rules (no eye gouging, biting, or groin strikes) along with no weight restrictions meant that the fighters squaring off would potentially be demonstrating how their individual arts would hold up on the street or in a combat situation.

Based on the Vale Tudo matches in Brazil, on November 12, 1993, UFC 1 took place in the now legendary Octagon™, a wire mesh cage designed to contain the ferocity of the fighters unleashing their skills against each other. That night, an anxious crowd gathered both in the McNichols Arena in Denver, Colorado—and nationwide in front of their television sets—unsure of what they might witness. Art Davie initially thought that Rickson Gracie should be the Gracie family representative instead of the eventual rep, Royce Gracie. Rickson was older, weighed more than the 175-pound Royce, and was generally considered to be the premier fighter of the clan. But after a disagreement with Rickson, Rorion deemed Royce the right choice for the match, stating that the smaller-framed fighter would better showcase the Gracie style.

By appearance alone, more conventional fighters such as kickboxer Pat Smith and shootfighter Ken Shamrock would appear to be favorites. But such predictions fell far short.

Royce defeated boxer Art Jimmerson; he just took him down and punched him a little bit and Jimmerson tapped out. A semifinal match between Royce and Ken Shamrock looked incredibly one-sided, with the 220-pound Shamrock the apparent favorite over his smaller foe. Instead, Royce rushed Shamrock, and after a brief struggle managed to get a gi choke on Shamrock, who tapped out, signaling defeat.

Royce's final match in UFC 1 was set against Dutch karate champion Gerard Gordeau. Gordeau fought Gracie while suffering from a broken hand sustained in his first-round match. Royce again took his opponent down and then quickly secured a rear naked choke for the victory. Against all expectations, Royce Gracie had demonstrated the effectiveness of the Gracie Jiu-Jitsu system, and he had done so on a sensational new sporting platform. Over 85,000 people watched the event on Pay-Per-View, instantly catapulting the event to superstar status.

To the audience watching and to fighters all over the world, the fact that Royce had managed to overcome a variety of opponents who seemed far superior (on paper at least) led to something of a wake-up call. The Gracie brothers were now in demand. People wanted to learn their techniques. In a short time, martial artists all over the world were asking themselves how they would handle the Gracie techniques.

Crazy for Gracie

In the wake of UFC 1, Royce Gracie would go on to win several more UFC matches before a no contest against Harold Howard in UFC 3. Dehydrated and exhausted after winning a grueling bout against Kimo Leopoldo, Gracie's corner threw in the towel shortly before his semifinal match was due to start.

Royce's setback did little to alter the fact that the martial arts world had fallen in love with groundfighting and grappling. Traditional striking-oriented arts fell out of favor as thousands flocked to gyms to learn how to handle themselves on the ground.

Official Gracie schools sprouted all over the world, offering students the chance to learn the famed "mount" position and every other tool in the Gracie arsenal. A video series was launched and the word "Gracie" became synonymous with groundfighting and grappling.

Eventually, as martial artists learned about the Gracie system and became familiar with the techniques, the strategic advantage lessened considerably. Strikers learned how to defend themselves against being taken down to the ground. Grapplers worked to include more strikes in their own arsenal. And rather than being lopsided practitioners, most fighters began evolving toward a balanced approach to fighting. They understood that there were three distinct aspects to any fight: standing, the clinch, and the takedown.

Notable Fights

(Photo courtesy Zuffa, LLC)

November 22, 2002: MGM Grand Arena, Las Vegas, Nevada

One of the most memorable grudge matches in combat sports history, the bout between Ken Shamrock and Tito Ortiz at UFC 40: Vendetta was one of the UFC's all-time highest-rated events. To this day, it remains an incredible fan favorite.

The two heated rivals immediately got down to business by trading punches at close range. Ortiz held an early edge, but a momentary lapse of judgment almost cost him the fight when he walked into a Shamrock right hook. Ortiz would briefly stagger, but he quickly regained his footing and his senses to finish the round strong.

Throughout round two, Ortiz landed thunderous strikes and delivered a volley of vicious elbows on the ground. By the end of round two, Shamrock was winded and his face showed the scars of battle.

Round three proved no better for Shamrock, who seemed to have no way of stopping the younger Ortiz' sustained attack. Only Shamrock's warrior's heart got him through the round. But at the start of round four, Shamrock's corner threw in the towel, conceding the match. The rivalry wasn't over yet, though, as the two would meet twice more in the Octagon, with Ortiz winning two more times.

As such, they worked to be able to hold their own during any one of those phases. As UFC matches progressed, more fighters entered the bouts hoping to test their mettle against others schooled in a variety of arts and techniques.

The UFC was gaining popularity, even as the dominance of groundfighters and their grappling skills waned slightly. But the UFC had bigger problems yet to be encountered.

Few Rules, Few Opportunities

The biggest problem the SEG organizers were encountering was a lack of public approval for the matches. While they had consistently shown that there was a readily identifiable audience for the events, the organizers had run afoul of a number of key figures.

Local and state governments, for one, were having trouble with the lack of rules imposed by the early UFC events. The apparent brutality of the fights being broadcast both shocked and appalled a number of regions, leading to a ban on the broadcasting of the events. Arizona's Senator John McCain even referred to the early UFC fights as little more than glorified "human cockfighting," a sentiment that further galvanized opposition to the organization.

> **FIGHTER FACTS**
>
> While Senator McCain initially proved to be one of the most outspoken critics of the early UFC, he would eventually soften his stance. When the UFC, under new leadership, integrated the unified rules and achieved sanctioning in many states, McCain re-evaluated his previous position.

The UFC's lack of rules also angered state athletic commissions, which hold great power when it comes to approving matches. Without a change in how the events were structured and run, the UFC was facing a serious problem. If they continued on their present course, they would shortly run out of places to broadcast the events from. As a result of that, advertising and sponsorships would quickly vanish.

The UFC as a profitable business venture would be a thing of the past unless its organizers found a way to maintain its base appeal while somehow giving the appearance of appeasing those the event had angered.

Instead of adapting to the political pressures and making the changes necessary to stay alive, the UFC resisted. Political pressure mounted on broadcasters, who saw little choice but to discontinue airing the UFC events. Pay-Per-View broadcasters, the UFC's monetary mainstay, dropped the events, and as a result, the UFC's public visibility dropped to virtually nothing. By 1995, Davie and Gracie had sold their stake in UFC to Semaphore Entertainment Group, their early partner for Pay-Per-View broadcasting. SEG continued to limp forward with the UFC. They worked with several state athletic commissions in an attempt to get the events cast more as sporting events rather than the brutal "spectacles" that its critics had branded it as.

There was still a long way to go.

From Black to White

By 2000, the California State Athletic Commission prepared rules with which to regulate mixed martial arts, but budgetary issues kept these rules from being implemented. New Jersey stepped up to the plate, though, behind commissioner Larry Hazzard, and became the first major state athletic commission to adopt the "Unified Rules of Mixed Martial Arts." UFC 28 on November 17, 2000, was the first UFC card to be sanctioned by the New Jersey State Athletic Commission (NJSAC).

But the battle for recognition had cost SEG dearly. Hovering on the brink of financial ruin, a trio that called themselves Zuffa, LLC approached SEG with an offer to buy the UFC brand. Dana White, a manager of fighters as well as owner of several boxing gyms, along with casino owner brothers Frank and Lorenzo Fertitta, comprised Zuffa, LLC. To them, the UFC was a diamond in the rough, badly needing the polish and enthusiasm that would turn their investment into a cash cow. The three partners were passionate about the brand, and they were hopeful that by making the right decisions and placing long-term success in front of short-term profits, in time, others would share their passion.

In January 2001, Zuffa, LLC took formal control of the UFC brand and immediately launched a proactive campaign to get the event on track to where it is today.

Zuffa's first order of business was getting the UFC sanctioned in Nevada. In early 2001, the UFC was officially sanctioned by the NSAC. And by UFC 33, the event staged its triumphant return to pay-per-view television, in Las Vegas no less.

Under the leadership of White and the Fertitta brothers, Zuffa propelled the UFC to greater heights than ever before. High-impact advertising and a dramatic increase in corporate sponsorship helped push the UFC's recognition factor higher. Additionally, the return to Pay-Per-View as well as a new home video distribution deal meant that the UFC was well on its way to achieving what Zuffa, LLC wanted it to be.

Pay-Per-View levels rose steadily as the events were broadcast from higher-profile platforms such as the Mandalay Bay Events Center and the MGM Grand Garden Arena. The UFC entered into deals with Fox Sports Net to showcase bouts from the UFC cards.

By UFC 40, the organization reached a restoration of its former glory since being pushed almost out of existence by political backlash. The match between Tito Ortiz and Ken Shamrock proved immensely successful. But even with its successes, the UFC was still not filling the coffers of Zuffa, LLC.

Clearly, something had to be done.

A Smashing Success

With American television viewers embedded in every reality show they could watch, White and the Fertitta brothers decided to test the waters with their own reality TV concept: *The Ultimate Fighter*. Brief exposure on the reality show *American Casino* had demonstrated that a TV series could effectively help them promote the UFC. As the idea was streamlined, Zuffa started pitching the idea to many of the networks but found only rejection.

Zuffa then approached the recently formed Spike TV with their idea for up-and-coming MMA fighters vying for top spots via competition bouts, with the goal of securing a six-figure UFC contract. Spike TV initially rejected the idea as well, but relented when Zuffa offered to put up $10 million in production costs. The reality, then, was that Zuffa wasn't so much launching a TV show as it was paying an enormous amount for advertising in the guise of reality TV.

In January 2005, *The Ultimate Fighter* launched and instantly became a runaway success. As a result, *The Ultimate Fighter* returned for season two in August 2005. 2006 saw two more runs, and additional seasons have been ordered for 2007 and 2008.

Spike TV has also launched several follow-up shows. *UFC Unleashed* is a weekly one-hour spot showcasing select fights from various UFC bouts. *UFC Fight Night* shows live UFC matches, serves as a promotional vehicle for upcoming UFC Pay-Per-View events, and reports on news affecting the entire UFC community. Also on Spike TV's lineup are *UFC Countdown* shows to Pay-Per-View events, and *UFC All-Access*, which takes viewers behind the scenes into a prominent athlete's life outside the Octagon.

The Ultimate Fighter *reality show on Spike TV is an amazing success.*

(Photo courtesy Zuffa, LLC)

Marc Ratner joined the UFC as Vice President of Regulatory Affairs in May of 2006. Ratner's previous position as the executive director of the Nevada State Athletic Commission had allied him with the political backlash against the UFC. But by joining the UFC in 2006, the signal was clear: the UFC was now a legitimate sporting event, worthy of the tremendous audience it was drawing into its legions of fans. Ratner's goals now are to help the UFC expand its scope to an international level, and ease its acceptance into regions where MMA events have not enjoyed sanctioning.

The UFC's future is undoubtedly a bright one.

New leadership for the UFC: Dana White.

(Photo courtesy Zuffa, LLC)

The Least You Need to Know

◆ Mixed martial arts is a combat sport dating back to ancient Greece, involving two competitors using striking and grappling techniques to defeat each other.

◆ *UFC 1: The Beginning* took place on November 12, 1993, in Denver, Colorado. Underdog Royce Gracie won, ushering in a new era of combat sports and a wave of Gracie Jiu-Jitsu fans.

◆ Despite the UFC's initial success, a lack of sanctioning and political backlash led to the UFC's "dark days" between 1997 and 2001.

◆ Zuffa, LLC purchased the UFC in 2001 and has subsequently turned it into a sports powerhouse.

Rules of the Octagon™

In This Chapter

- The Nevada State Athletic Commission
- Mandatory Equipment
- Weight Classes
- Time Limits and Rounds
- Fouls
- Referee Intervention

The Ultimate Fighting Championship® emerged from its self-described "dark ages," a period during which sponsorships and advertisers waned to the point that the UFC® was in serious jeopardy of disappearing completely, to rapidly assert itself as a premier sporting event. Its Phoenix-like rebirth was due to one simple thing: sanctioning.

When Zuffa, LLC bought the UFC brand in 2001, their first order of business was to get the events sanctioned in Nevada, the fight capital of the world and host to the world's biggest boxing events. In order to do that, they needed to prove that mixed martial arts wasn't a barbaric spectacle, but a legitimate sport that had already adopted unified rules, had been sanctioned in New Jersey, and had placed fighter safety as its paramount concern.

Zuffa, LLC, under the direction of Dana White and the Fertitta brothers, took on this task, looking to bring MMA to the masses.

In this chapter, we take a look at exactly how the UFC shook itself free of its former darker pit-fighting image and transformed itself into a sanctioned organization with rules, weight classes, time limits, and all the other trappings of traditional sporting events.

Getting Sanctioned

Zuffa, LLC knew that if they hoped to have any chance at success, they would have to align themselves with state athletic commissions. In order to do this, they had to show a willingness to follow rules that would elevate the UFC's status in the eyes of state governing bodies. Adopting a system of unified rules would help show that the UFC was interested in protecting the safety of its fighters, as well as its impact on society at large.

The undisputed capital of mixed martial arts training was California. The Gracie family had settled there and in the wake of the first UFC, many other MMA camps had taken root throughout the state as well. Despite the obvious popularity of the training, competitions in the state were illegal.

Since the late 1990s, MMA pioneers had tried to get the state to recognize a set of rules that they hoped would open the door to legal events. The California State Athletic Commission finally appeared to accept a new set of "unified rules" on April 28, 2000, but instead of immediately heralding a new wave of events, the commission ran out of money and could not move forward.

Instead of enduring purgatory, the New Jersey State Athletic Commission's executive director, Larry Hazzard, agreed to test these new rules out in an event that occurred on September 30, 2000. While the show itself got scant notice from anyone, Hazzard liked what he saw. After a few more tweaks to the rules, UFC 28 took place at the Taj Mahal on November 15, 2000. The show was a spectacular success, and in April of 2001, the UFC's new owners, Zuffa, LLC, along with other MMA promoters and enthusiasts, met with Hazzard and the New Jersey State Athletic Commission and ironed out the final version of what soon after became mixed martial arts' unified rules of conduct.

Having proved that a UFC that played by the new unified rules could be a success, Zuffa, LLC next sought sanctioning in the nation's playground: Las Vegas.

Also known as NSAC, the Nevada State Athletic Commission is the governing body that regulates all aspects of combat sports in the state of Nevada. It also has the power of regulation over licensing, promotion, management, and other tangential relationships to the world of combat sports. With over 38 million people visiting Las Vegas every year, acquiring sanctioning by NSAC would position the UFC in a very profitable area. NSAC is also viewed as the premier state athletic commissioning body in the United States. Getting an official nod from them would certainly open doors in other states as well.

PRO-FILES   **Chuck "The Iceman" Liddell**

(Photo courtesy Zuffa, LLC)

Fighting out of: San Luis Obispo, California
Born: 12/17/69
Height: 6'2"
Weight: 205 lbs.
Weightclass: Light Heavyweight, former UFC Light Heavyweight Champion

Born and raised in California, Chuck is best known for his amazing striking skills, including the most feared right hand in mixed martial arts history. Also known for his stellar takedown defense and his trademark mohawk, the soft-spoken "Iceman"'s recent notable fights include a third-round technical knockout over Tito Ortiz in December 2006. One of the notable times Chuck lost in the Octagon was back in 2003 when he was stopped in the third round by Randy Couture at *UFC 43: Meltdown*—a loss he later avenged twice. According to Chuck, "I just want to keep fighting and winning."

By abiding by the new unified rules, the UFC was sending a clear signal not just to NSAC, but to all state athletic commissions: we want to be recognized and sanctioned and we're willing to do what you say to accomplish this goal.

As a result of the UFC's sanctioning in New Jersey and Nevada, as well as its commitment to maintaining the highest standards and adherence to the unified rules, California, Texas, Ohio, Florida, and Louisiana have also sanctioned UFC events. In fact, UFC events are now sanctioned in 24 states.

Gearing Up

As part of the unified rules that the UFC now abides by, fighters in the Octagon must wear certain mandatory equipment.

Chief among this equipment are gloves that weigh four ounces. This is far less than the eight- or ten-ounce gloves typically worn by boxers. The gloves worn by UFC fighters are intended to protect the hands of the fighters.

> **Surface area** is a term used to designate exactly how much of a given surface is used to strike. In the case of gloves worn in the UFC, the minimal four-ounce does not pad the fist/hand much beyond its natural state. By contrast, the eight- and ten-ounce gloves worn in boxing significantly enlarge the hands of the fighters, making it easier to land blows than in MMA, where greater accuracy is required.

Also unlike boxing, the gloves worn by UFC fighters have finger separations that enable them to grapple with opponents and apply submissions and chokes in the course of the match. The smaller gloves worn by UFC fighters also make it far easier to score knockouts and inflict damage. It's interesting to note that medical research has shown a single knockout is far less destructive to the brain than a fighter who endures round after round of successive pounding shots to his head.

Beyond the gloves, the only other mandatory equipment is MMA shorts or kickboxing trunks, a groin protector, and mouthpiece. Unlike its early days, UFC fighters are no longer permitted to wear traditional "GI" uniforms, tops, shirts, or shoes. Aside from the dangers these clothes pose for fighters, they also give opponents an unfair advantage.

By limiting the amount of equipment, the playing field for both competitors is leveled to the extent that the fight remains what it was intended to be: a bout between two relatively similar fighters, with the best warrior winning the bout.

Weighing In

While the UFC had used certain weight classes prior to adopting the unified rules, they were quite different from what is in place today. In order to achieve their sanctioning goals, the UFC had to abide by weight class rules that more closely resembled boxing.

New weight divisions for the UFC have helped get it sanctioned in many states.

(Photo courtesy Zuffa, LLC)

The UFC, in meeting with Larry Hazzard of the New Jersey State Athletic Commission in April 2001, had agreed to weight classes as stipulated in the new unified rules. The UFC now had to ensure its fighters were all in bouts against fighters of similar weight.

These days, the UFC fighters fall into five separate weight classes.

- **Lightweight.** Fighters falling into this weight class must weigh at least 145 pounds. They may not exceed 155 pounds when they weigh in prior to a competition.

- **Welterweight.** The next class up, fighters must be over 155 pounds but may not exceed 170 pounds at the pre-fight weigh-in.

- **Middleweight.** UFC fighters in the middleweight class must be over 170 pounds but may not weigh more than 185 pounds when they step on the scales before the battle.

> **FIGHTER FACTS**
>
> Other mixed martial arts venues feature a featherweight division for fighters who weigh up to 145 pounds and a super heavyweight division for fighters who weigh more than 265 pounds. The UFC currently does not have these weight classes.

◆ **Light Heavyweight.** Fighting in this weight class means that fighters must weigh more than 185 pounds but they may not exceed 205 pounds at the weigh-in.

◆ **Heavyweight.** The big boys of the bunch, the heavyweight fighters must be heavier than 205 pounds but may not weigh more than 265 pounds at the pre-fight weigh-in.

The introduction of weight classes has helped the UFC improve its image considerably as a sporting venue. At the same time, the introduction of weight classes has also shown that the UFC is committed to the safety of its fighters. By pairing warriors of similar weight with one another, the chances of injury and outright mismatches are slight. And that means a better event for everyone involved.

FIGHTER FACTS

There can be a significant weight difference in fighters between when they weigh in and when the actual fight takes place. Some commissions stipulate that fighters must weigh in no longer than 24 hours prior to a match, so fighters have been known to drop their weight sharply in order to meet their weight class requirements, only to suddenly bulk up immediately after the weigh-in, using their increased size to their advantage in the Octagon.

Working with the Clock

Another key factor of the unified rules to which the UFC agreed to abide by was the introduction of rounds during all events. As such, all UFC sanctioned events consist of the following:

◆ Nonchampionship events consist of three rounds. Each of the three rounds lasts for five minutes.

◆ Championship bouts consist of five rounds, with each one lasting five minutes.

◆ In between each round is a one-minute rest period, during which time fighters return to their respective areas of the Octagon for water, coaching, and help from their cut-men.

As with the introduction of weight classes, the establishment of rounds and time periods has helped the UFC's quest to be a viable platform for combat sports.

Notable Fights

(Photo courtesy Zuffa, LLC)

April 16, 2005: MGM Grand Arena, Las Vegas, Nevada

In a welterweight championship match between reigning champ Matt Hughes and challenger Frank Trigg, tensions escalated early on when Trigg nailed Hughes with an accidental knee strike to the groin. When Hughes turned to complain to the referee, Trigg moved in fast.

The referee had not seen the groin shot and didn't call a foul. But more importantly, Hughes suddenly had to deal with a barrage of strikes unleashed by Trigg, who then attempted a rear naked choke submission.

Hughes, in spectacular fashion, escaped from what looked to be an unshakable choke, literally picked Trigg up and slammed him back down to the mat on the other side of the Octagon.

After a brief scuffle on the ground, Hughes quickly secured Trigg in his own rear naked choke. Trigg had no choice but to tap out. Coincidentally enough, Hughes had used this exact same technique to finish off Trigg in their first match against one another.

Hughes retained his welterweight championship as a result of winning. But he also pulled off what many experts consider to be the most amazing comeback in UFC history.

Crying Foul

Early UFC fights had few moves that could be considered fouls. These days, the UFC has some strict guidelines on what is permitted in the course of the action. We take a look at the entire list of things that a UFC fighter can be penalized for doing during a fight.

UFC fighters are not allowed to headbutt their opponents deliberately. In the course of the fight, there may be accidental contact, but the referee has the final say over whether it was incidental or deliberate.

No eye gouging of any kind is allowed under the Unified Rules of Mixed Martial Arts. Obviously, attacks to the eyes are considered vicious and debilitating. As such, they are not permitted.

A fighter is checked for injuries between rounds by the referee, cutman, and Octagonside physician.

(Photo courtesy Zuffa, LLC)

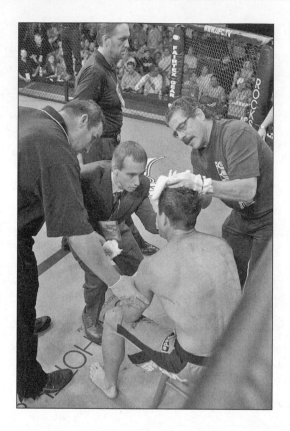

Biting is strictly forbidden. Along with the rather barbaric nature of such attacks, the human mouth is capable of transmitting many forms of infectious bacteria. Fighters resorting to biting will find themselves without a future in the UFC.

Fighters may not pull the hair of their opponent. Most UFC fighters, realizing that hair can actually be a vulnerability even with hair pulling outlawed, choose to wear their locks cut extremely short. Others choose to shave their heads entirely.

Fish hooking—the act by which a fighter inserts his finger into a soft tissue area and then pulls an opponent down—is strictly prohibited. Common fish hooking involves using the index finger to snag the inside of a person's cheek and then yank them down from there.

Likewise, UFC fighters are banned from using their fingers to poke cuts or lacerations or otherwise insert their fingers into any orifice on the opposing fighter.

UFC fighters may not engage in small joint manipulation. Small joints in this case refers to fingers and toes.

Due to the devastating nature of such strikes, UFC fighters may not hit the spine or the back of another fighter's head.

Downward elbow strikes, from the ceiling to the floor or from 12 o'clock to 6 o'clock in motion, are also forbidden under the unified rules.

Throat strikes are also not permitted during UFC bouts.

Clawing attacks or twisting another fighter's flesh is not allowed during UFC bouts. This also includes any type of skin pinch.

Due to the ease by which it may break, UFC fighters are banned from grabbing an opponent's clavicle.

Fighters may not knee strike an opponent in the head if they are "grounded" (on the ground, as might be seen during a takedown or submission).

They may not kick the head of a grounded opponent, either.

Fighters may not stomp a grounded opponent. "Stomping" in this case would refer to the act of lifting a leg and driving it down vertically with the heel to inflict damage.

Kicks to the kidney using the heel are also forbidden. (This might typically be seen during the course of the match when one fighter is maneuvering on top of another fighter and the fighter underneath has his legs locked around the waist of the fighter on top.)

FIGHTER FACTS

Fighters who violate these rules can be disqualified from the fight. Repeat offenders who routinely disregard the rules and engage in unsportsmanlike conduct may have their punishments escalated by the State Athletic Commission.

"Spiking" is forbidden. Spiking is the act of driving an opponent into the ground head or neck first. This is obviously a dangerous attack and could easily result in serious injury.

Fighters are not allowed to throw an opponent out of the ring or fenced area. Such attacks would be considered extreme.

UFC fighters are not permitted to latch on to or otherwise hold the gloves or shorts of another fighter.

Spitting is forbidden.

Unsportsmanlike conduct is not tolerated in the Octagon, especially if that conduct then results in injury to an opponent.

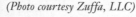

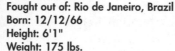

UFC LEGENDS **Hall of Famer: Royce Gracie**

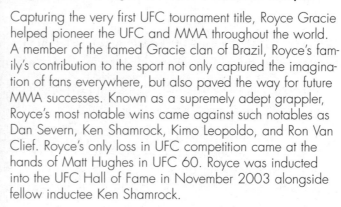

(Photo courtesy Zuffa, LLC)

Fought out of: Rio de Janeiro, Brazil
Born: 12/12/66
Height: 6'1"
Weight: 175 lbs.
Weightclass: Middleweight Three-time UFC Tournament Champion

Capturing the very first UFC tournament title, Royce Gracie helped pioneer the UFC and MMA throughout the world. A member of the famed Gracie clan of Brazil, Royce's family's contribution to the sport not only captured the imagination of fans everywhere, but also paved the way for future MMA successes. Known as a supremely adept grappler, Royce's most notable wins came against such notables as Dan Severn, Ken Shamrock, Kimo Leopoldo, and Ron Van Clief. Royce's only loss in UFC competition came at the hands of Matt Hughes in UFC 60. Royce was inducted into the UFC Hall of Fame in November 2003 alongside fellow inductee Ken Shamrock.

During the midst of the bout, fighters may not hold the fence. Doing so would allow one fighter to better position himself.

Abusive language, not limited to profanity, is not permitted in the ring or fenced areas of UFC bouts.

A UFC fighter may not attack an opponent during a break between rounds or a fighter who is otherwise on respite.

Fighters may not attack an opponent who is being looked after by the referee.

Fighters are not permitted to attack an opponent after the bell has sounded, which signals the end of a round.

UFC fighters are reminded to obey the instructions of the referee at all times. Disregarding a referee's instructions is forbidden.

UFC fighters must at all times show an aggressive nature in the midst of a fight. Any displays of retreat or timidity are prohibited. Pretending to be injured, dropping the mouthpiece deliberately, and consistent lack of aggression are grounds for a foul.

FIGHTER FACTS

Fighters are encouraged to be aggressive, but that doesn't mean they are in a blind rage. As long as they confidently try to achieve their wins through a sustained, smart offense, they will not be charged with a lack of aggression.

Today's UFC is a far different venue than it was early on. With rules like the above in place, the UFC has shown a willingness to protect its fighters while simultaneously enhancing the nature of its events.

Getting the Referee Involved

The referee of a UFC match has a great deal of power. He ensures the safety of the fighters and makes certain they adhere to the rules of the Octagon.

The referee also ensures that fighters are continuously striving to best their opponents. If a situation arises on the ground or against the fence in the clinch where neither fighter is actively seeking an end to the fight or the action has lulled and neither is in danger of being stopped by strikes or a submission, the referee can restart the fighters, on their feet, in the center of the Octagon

Big John McCarthy has presided over many of the UFC's most memorable bouts.

(Photo courtesy Zuffa, LLC)

The referee must also be on the lookout for any sign of serious injury in either fighter. If he sees one fighter unable to intelligently defend himself or otherwise injured too seriously, the referee may stop the fight.

The referee may also direct the fight doctor to examine a fighter he believes is injured in order to make a better judgment about that fighter's ability to continue the match.

Put simply, the referee is the hawk that watches every aspect of the action, working to ensure safety and sportsmanship are preserved through strict adherence to the rules.

The Least You Need to Know

◆ Shortly after acquiring the brand, Zuffa, LLC got the UFC sanctioned in Nevada. The UFC was reborn.

◆ UFC fighters wear four-ounce gloves and MMA shorts or kickboxing trunks as mandatory equipment.

◆ There are five weight classes in the UFC: lightweight, welterweight, middleweight, light heavyweight, and heavyweight.

◆ Nonchampionship bouts have three five-minute rounds. Championship bouts have five five-minute rounds. There is a one-minute rest break between all rounds.

◆ The unified rules list 31 separate causes for fouls during a competition.

◆ Referees are an integral part of making sure UFC bouts are as safe as possible for the fighters involved.

3

And the Winner Is ...

In This Chapter

♦ The Octagon™

♦ Knockouts

♦ Submissions

♦ Technical Knockouts

♦ Decisions

♦ Forfeits, Disqualifications, and No Contest

After the long road of competing in smaller events, learning techniques, perfecting strategies, endless workouts, lifting weights, running, and eating right, the event is at long last here. Now it's time to put everything they've worked for on the line. As they prepare to enter the Octagon, the fighters know one thing with absolute certainty:

Two will enter.

One will leave victorious.

In this chapter, we take a look at exactly how these modern-day gladiators become champions in the UFC®. As unique as each fighter is, as varied as their backgrounds and training may be, there are only a few ways they can prevail.

The road to victory lies before them. And each fighter wants it. Bad.

Welcome to the Octagon

Before a fighter can attempt to best another, he must first contend with the awesome arena constructed for Ultimate Fighting Championship® battles. Since its inception, the UFC's only venue for bouts has been the Octagon.

This is where it all happens ....

(Photo courtesy Zuffa, LLC)

Now synonymous with the great events put on by the UFC, the Octagon remains one of its most lasting and perennial images. The eight-sided arena features a wraparound fence coated with black vinyl approximately six feet high. The edges are padded to help ensure fighter safety.

The Octagon stands four feet above the normal surface of the floor. Special padding underneath the mat helps protect the fighters, although taking a fall on the padded canvas can still hurt!

The Octagon's competition surface is 30 feet across. There are two entry points to the Octagon, but these are closed during the match itself, ensuring that fighters will not be at risk from falling out of the competition area, which has happened in a traditional ring due to the grappling aspect of the sport.

The floor of the Octagon normally features sponsorship advertisements, which are changed before each event.

The World of Knockouts

For most people, the word "knockout" comes from the world of boxing, which has long popularized the term. Boxers have used jabs, crosses, hooks, and uppercuts to successfully knock out their opponents.

Nowadays, UFC fighters are doing it as well.

Fighters looking to score a knockout victory do so by using their limbs to strike their opponents in either the head or the body. These strikes then render the opponent unable to continue and the fight is over.

A knockout in action.

(Photo courtesy Zuffa, LLC)

Knockouts can come from a single punch, applied just right at the correct spot on the opponent's anatomy. Or the knockout may come as a result of successive strikes whose damage culminates over time, reducing the opponent's ability to withstand or absorb the impacts. UFC fighters have scored spectacular knockouts in the past. Kicks to the head, a barrage of punches, vicious body blows, and a variety of other striking techniques have all granted knockout victories to many of the UFC's best warriors.

PRO-FILES   *Anderson "The Spider" Silva*

(Photo courtesy Zuffa, LLC)

Fighting out of: Curitiba, Brazil
Born: 4/14/75
Height: 6'2"
Weight: 185 lbs.
Weightclass: Middleweight
UFC Middleweight Champion

A veteran of many martial arts styles, Anderson is known for his intense training regimen, as well as for his incredible striking power. With a background in Tae Kwon Do, Muay Thai, and grappling, Anderson, a Brazilian Jiu-Jitsu black belt, is very well rounded. His first two UFC wins came in the form of a knockout scored 43 seconds into the first round of *UFC Fight Night 5* against Chris Leben in June 2006 and a technical knockout win against Rich Franklin at UFC 64 in October 2006 to win the UFC Middleweight title. But he showed his overall game in February 2007 as he submitted fellow Jiu-Jitsu black belt Travis Lutter in the second round.

Submit, Submit, Submit

Since the UFC and MMA in general incorporate not just striking, but also grappling, fighters also have the option of taking their opponents to the ground and forcing them to "submit."

Getting the submission.

(Photo courtesy Zuffa, LLC)

Submissions can either involve the application of a choke hold or wrenching a joint in such a way as to produce an incredible amount of pain. In the event that a UFC fighter successfully locks up his opponent, there are two ways the soon-to-be-defeated can signal his intent to concede: the verbal tap out and the more common physical tap out.

Verbal Tap Out

A fighter who finds himself in an undesirable and inescapable position may signal his concession by verbally informing the referee that he is finished. The referee will immediately move in to stop the fight, thereby ensuring the safety of the fighter who has lost. A verbal tap out would be most commonly seen when a submission other than a choke hold is used. Armbars, leg locks, and certain other submissions would enable an opponent to verbally signal his concession.

Physical Tap Out

A choke hold, on the other hand, is likely to restrict the opponent's ability to signal his intent verbally. Choke holds can be applied to restrict blood flow to the head, resulting in unconsciousness. In either event, the fighter who finds himself trapped in a choke hold or other submission hold is far more likely to signal his concession by tapping the mat or his opponent's body three times in rapid succession. This tap-tap-tap immediately signals the referee to stop the fight. If the fighter taps his opponent's body, the fighter applying the hold must immediately stop and withdraw, allowing the referee access to the defeated fighter to check on his well-being.

Technically, It's a Knockout

A technical knockout, or TKO, as it's better known, is another avenue by which UFC fighters may win their bouts. A TKO victory can be achieved in one of three ways: referee, doctor, or corner stoppages.

Referee Stoppage

The UFC referee has the option of stopping the fight at any time if one or more of the following occurs:

- One fighter establishes himself as dominant and his opponent is unable to intelligently defend himself from repeated attacks, which might lead to excessive injury if not stopped. There is no minimum time limit on this action; a referee may stop the fight if it is immediately evident that one fighter is totally outclassed by the other.

A referee stops the fight.

(Photo courtesy Zuffa, LLC)

- ◆ If during a groundfighting situation one of the fighters becomes unconscious due to a submission hold, the referee will immediately stop the fight to limit further damage to the unconscious fighter and will award a submission win to the victor.

- ◆ If over the course of the fight one fighter appears to have a significant number of injuries, or if a particular injury appears to be worsening to the point that the fighter's health is being exponentially compromised, the referee will stop the fight.

Doctor Stoppage

If during the course of the fight the referee doubts one fighter's ability to continue due to injury or a cut, the referee will call for a time out. During the time out, the fight doctor will inspect the fighter in question and advise the referee as to whether the fight should be allowed to continue.

If the fight doctor advises the referee that the fighter in question is unfit to continue, the referee will make the final decision whether or not the fight should be stopped and the opponent declared the winner.

If the fight is stopped by the referee due to injury caused by an illegal move or technique, however, the offending fighter will either be disqualified or a "no contest" judgment will be issued.

After two rounds in a nonchampionship or three rounds in a championship fight, if the referee judges that an accidental foul has occurred and the fight must be stopped, then the result goes to the judges for a decision.

An invaluable asset, a good cutman can save the fight.

(Photo courtesy Zuffa, LLC)

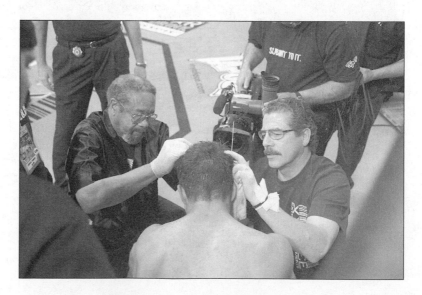

Corner Stoppage

If a fighter's corner—including his trainer/coach, cutmen, etc.—feel that their fighter is in serious jeopardy, the corner may stop the fight between rounds. They may also throw a towel into the ring or cage to signify they are conceding defeat, but technically this would result in a foul under Nevada rules, due to corner interference. A fighter's corner may well be a better judge of whether the fighter can continue or not, rather than the fighter himself knowing or trying to weather unnecessary damage.

FIGHTSPEAK

Cutmen use a cold metal bar called an Enswell pressed against bruises to try to alleviate excessive swelling; cotton swabs are used to apply direct pressure to bleeding cuts; Vaseline and commission-approved liniments are applied to the face to reduce friction cuts. All of these techniques are designed to enable a fighter to continue as long as possible and to hopefully avoid the referee stoppage.

The Deciding Factor

If both fighters are able to endure the punishment of going the distance of either three or five rounds, the judges will then determine the winner of the fight by using the points they have tallied on their score cards.

Under the current rules in place at UFC events, the "10-point must" system is in effect. This means that the fighter judged to win the round must be awarded 10 points. The loser of the round can be awarded no more than 9 points. If the round is judged to be even, both fighters are awarded 10 points. In most situations, a losing fighter can receive no fewer than 7 points per round.

FIGHTER FACTS

While many fans believe that the UFC itself has control over the judges who score bouts, the fact is, they do not. Judges are chosen by the state athletic commission of whatever state that particular UFC bout is being held in. And while most of the judges working UFC bouts in the early days of the unified rules were actually boxing judges who had little to no experience judging a mixed martial arts match, that's not always the case today, when many judges are well versed in the craft and techniques of MMA.

Unanimous Decision

A unanimous decision is one in which all three judges have scored the bout in favor of one fighter.

Split Decision

When the judges are not all in agreement about who they think the winner should be, the ruling is called a split decision. This would be the case if two of the judges think that fighter A should win and the third judge believes that fighter B won the fight.

Majority Decision

When two of the judges score the bout in favor of fighter A, but the third judge believes the fight should be scored a draw, the ruling is called a majority decision.

Draw

In the unlikely event that all three judges score the match even after the three or five rounds, the match itself will be declared a draw. Draws may also occur when one judge votes for each fighter, with the third calling the bout even, or when two judges see the fight even, with the third voting for one of the two fighters. Draws are an abnormal occurrence in the UFC, with most bouts being decided one way or another. But there always exists the possibility that two fighters may be so evenly matched and talented that they are able to fight to a total standstill.

Disqualifications

While rare, disqualifications do happen from time to time. Fighters who ignore the established rules that govern UFC matches will be given a warning. Repeated warnings will usually result in a disqualification, but this is at the referee's discretion.

Additionally, if a fighter is injured and no longer able to continue the fight due to an intentional foul, the offending fighter is disqualified and the injured fighter declared the winner of the match.

During UFC 43, Wes Sims was disqualified during his match with Frank Mir. Sims had just escaped an armbar and threw Mir down to the mat. Rather than submit Mir using legal techniques, Sims started stomping on Mir's head. The fight was stopped but Mir was unable to continue. As a result, Sims was disqualified and Mir declared the winner.

Notable Fights

(Photo courtesy Zuffa, LLC)

June 6, 2003: Thomas and Mack Center, Las Vegas, Nevada

Over 9,000 fans watched a startling upset as clear underdog Randy Couture defeated Chuck Liddell via a third-round technical knockout to win the interim UFC Light Heavyweight title.

Despite being just days away from his fortieth birthday at the time of the fight, Couture came out strong and prepared to take on the famed blitzkrieg strikes of Liddell. In fact, Couture, a world-class wrestler, surprised many by holding his own against Liddell as they traded punches.

As round two opened, Couture's own assault began wearing Liddell down and he repeatedly beat "The Iceman" to the punch. As the round wore on, it was becoming apparent that Liddell was having trouble dealing with Couture.

Couture finished things off in round three, by softening Liddell up with another barrage of strikes prior to getting a takedown and rapidly assuming the mount position. As he prepared to unleash another volley of punches, the referee stepped in and declared Couture the winner.

No Contest

If both fighters employ illegal techniques, or otherwise violate the rules, the fight will end with a "no contest" judgment. A no contest can occur if a fighter cannot continue due to an unintentional foul within the first two rounds of a nonchampionship fight and within the first three rounds of a championship fight.

A more common cause for a "no contest" judgment occurs when a fighter is injured or cut by an accidental illegal technique and is unable to continue fighting. Judges and officials know that accidental illegal strikes and techniques do sometimes happen.

> **UFC LEGENDS** **Hall of Famer: Ken Shamrock**
>
> *(Photo courtesy Zuffa, LLC)*
>
> **Fought out of: La Jolla, California**
> **Born: 2/11/64**
> **Height: 6'0"**
> **Weight: 205 lbs.**
> **Weightclass: Light Heavyweight**
> **UFC Superfight Champion**
>
> After losing to Royce Gracie in UFC 1, Ken Shamrock became the first fighter to actually battle Gracie to a draw in *UFC 5: Return of the Beast*. Thereafter, Ken had a series of wins and losses as he tussled with some of the best fighters trying to make a name for themselves in the UFC. Known for his submission skills, Ken is also a solid striker. Ken's notable wins include two victories over Kimo Leopoldo and over fellow Hall of Famer Dan Severn. He may be best remembered for his three-fight series against Tito Ortiz, with whom Ken has had an antagonistic relationship throughout his career. And though Ken lost that trilogy of bouts, his warrior's heart has never been questioned. Ken continues to run his Lions Den gym for mixed martial artists and he is concentrating on training a new generation of gladiators for MMA bouts.

The Least You Need to Know

- The Octagon is an eight-sided arena with a 30-foot competition area, fencing, and padding, where all UFC bouts are fought.

- Knockouts may be scored with single or multiple strikes.

- Submission victories can be scored with choke holds or other submission holds. A fighter wishing to concede may verbally submit, or tap the mat or the opponent's body three times in rapid succession.

- Technical knockouts are scored by way of a referee stoppage, a doctor stoppage, or a corner stoppage.

- The UFC uses a "10-point must" system of scoring and decisions can take the form of unanimous, split, majority, or draw verdicts.

- Disqualifications and no-contest rulings, though rare, do happen from time to time in UFC bouts.

Part 2

Today's Ultimate Fighter™ Athlete

What does it take to be a UFC fighter? In this part, we look at the basic styles of martial arts that make up the core of the UFC fighters. We also examine the various fighting strategies of today's top Octagon™ contenders and how each one has its own strengths and weaknesses.

4

The New Breed of Gladiators

In This Chapter

- ◆ Putting the "Mixed" Back in MMA
- ◆ Boxing
- ◆ Kickboxing
- ◆ Wrestling
- ◆ Jiu-Jitsu
- ◆ Judo

The early years of the UFC® were predominantly the playing field of fighters who specialized in one style of fighting. The idea of "mixing" martial arts styles applied to the bouts themselves, rather than the fighters mixing their own skills with those of other arts. A Karate stylist would fight a wrestler in the Octagon™. That was about as far as "mixing" went.

But an interesting thing happened on the way to the mat. When Royce Gracie introduced the world to his family's brand of Jiu-Jitsu, and striking specialists got a taste of groundfighting and vice versa, the UFC fighters and MMA fighters in general started exploring ways they could integrate the techniques of other arts into their own.

By doing so, they exponentially increased the tools available in their arsenal. Fighters got more complex in their strategies. They became more well rounded and better able to handle the myriad situations that could unfold within the Octagon.

It was, virtually, a case of the old candy commercial for Reese's Peanut Butter Cups. The "you-got-your-chocolate-in-my-peanut-butter/you-got-your-peanut-butter-on-my-chocolate" lines were edited. Chocolate and peanut butter became striking and groundfighting.

It was a true sense of evolution. By themselves, striking and grappling, while formidable, could never hope to achieve lasting success. Each needed the complementary aspects of the other in order to produce fighters able to provide UFC's growing fan base with the sport they wanted to see.

In this chapter, we take a look at the most popular styles today's fighters choose to study. And we'll examine how they've adapted these styles to suit their needs within the Octagon.

Mixing It Up

The base skills needed for mixed martial arts were undoubtedly the arts that emphasized striking and the arts that focused on groundfighting. What made Royce Gracie's win in UFC 1 so utterly nuclear was the fact that most of the fans watching this new sport venue were conditioned to the supposed superiority of striking. The fans knew about boxing. Even non-pugilists have caught snippets of boxing matches on TV. Popular boxers have become household names over the years. And no doubt, when news of the UFC started prior to the event, most of those tuning in expected to see strikers fare far better than the groundfighters.

Imagine, then, their shock when Royce Gracie, using very little striking, managed to take out not one, but two very skilled strikers on his way to becoming the first champion. What was going on? Why hadn't the strikers been able to simply catch him with a hook or an uppercut?

In the wake of UFC 1, the fighting world realized that they had grossly underestimated the capabilities of wrestlers, Jiu-Jitsu and Judo practitioners, and other groundfighters.

Simultaneously, the groundfighters realized that while they had emerged relatively unscathed in the first UFC competition, going in without a smattering of striking skills was probably not the smartest thing to do.

The striker.

(Photo courtesy Zuffa, LLC)

The cross-pollination of these two disciplines began in earnest. Strikers started studying Gracie and Brazilian Jiu-Jitsu. Other strikers went back to their high school wrestling lessons. Groundfighters started strapping on gloves and hitting the heavy bag, trying to learn how to deliver punches and kicks that could actually do damage.

It's somewhat taken for granted nowadays, that UFC fighters are naturally well-versed in both striking and groundfighting. But only about a decade ago, it was considered revolutionary to study both disciplines.

The grappler.

(Photo courtesy Zuffa, LLC)

Today's men of the Octagon are constantly on the lookout for ways to integrate new techniques into their fighting style. Most of them train with a number of coaches. In the Octagon today, fighters have learned that it truly is unwise to place all of your eggs in one basket.

The "Sweet Science" of Boxing

Distilled from the bare-knuckle competitions that sprang up throughout Europe from about the eighteenth century on, boxing truly came into its own in the twentieth century. Using a limited number of punches combined with footwork, boxers look to outstrike their opponents. Early boxers wore minimally padded gloves while today's exponents use eight- or ten- ounce gloves designed to protect the hands and increase the surface area of their punches.

Boxing's value to UFC fighters and mixed martial artists in general can best be illustrated by how a boxer uses his hands to set up combinations that enable him to bridge the distance between himself and his opponent. These punches build on the openings that each provides. In boxing, a jab may cause the opponent to alter his position, unknowingly placing himself into optimal range for a cross. That cross may then set up a perfect hook that leads to a knockout. In MMA, the left hook may leave an opening for a right kick to the body. Incorporating the strikes of boxing into a UFC fighter's arsenal just gives the athlete more tools to work with.

UFC fighters can benefit from boxing's footwork to a degree. Watching old matches shows the importance of keeping feet aligned with an opponent's *centerline* in order to deliver the maximum amount of impact force from strikes. When strikers learn to coordinate their feet and hands along the same lines of travel, the potential for truly devastating hits is magnified greatly.

FIGHTSPEAK

The **centerline** is an imaginary line that runs down the middle of an opponent's body. By learning how to deliver strikes that hit along this line, a fighter can maximize the damage his strikes cause. Knowing how to affect the centerline of an opponent is also useful in takedowns and throws.

Boxing also teaches the importance of a fighter keeping his hands up. Boxers learn to use their posture to help ward off an opponent's punches. In today's UFC matches, fighters rapidly learn that if they do not work to minimize their own openings, an opponent will be only too happy to exploit them.

For fighters who have never practiced a striking art and still aspire to enter the UFC, boxing is one of the best ways to rapidly acquire a baseline in punching techniques. Boxing techniques are at once simple and complex. But fighters can easily assimilate its teachings and then use those teachings to improve their own chances in the Octagon. Mixed martial artists must remember, though, that all boxing techniques aren't applicable in the Octagon. For example, boxers are taught to plant their feet before throwing power shots. In mixed martial arts, that technique can result in a superior grappler putting you on your back. Yet another example is traditional bobbing and weaving to avoid punches, which can leave a fighter painfully vulnerable to kicks and knees. So you must carefully pick and choose what you take from the sweet science in order to succeed.

Getting Your Kicks

Kickboxers have married boxing concepts to the use of the legs and feet as striking tools. UFC fighters specializing in kickboxing typically have experience in American Kickboxing, or the Thai art of Muay Thai. Many fighters also start out as children taking part in more traditional martial arts such as Tae Kwon Do or karate. Now, along with the benefits of hand strikes, fighters have the option of using feet, elbows, shins, and knees to strike their opponents. And while hand strikes can be devastating, properly delivered kicks can generate many times more power and devastation than their smaller counterparts.

In today's UFC, fighters appreciate the strategic advantage that kicks provide. They offer the opportunity to reach out at a further distance and strike than is afforded the hands. In an Octagon that is 30 feet across, a kick that has been properly set up can end the fight before it even starts.

And many UFC fighters, like Chuck Liddell, have scored awesome knockouts using a roundhouse kick to the head of an opponent. A fighter like UFC veteran Pedro Rizzo prefers to keep his kicks lower, lashing out at the legs of his opponents. There are enough people who have experienced the power of a Rizzo leg kick to know that they are extremely effective, mainly because after taking a few of them, walking and throwing your own kicks or even planting your foot to throw a punch becomes an exercise in painful futility.

In close, knees can be brought into play. Particularly in the clinch, fighters can wrap their hands around the head of their opponent and using that as leverage, bring their knees up into the face repeatedly. If the fighter on the receiving end of those knee strikes does not get himself out of there, he may well end up having his face rearranged and losing the fight.

Kickboxing has definitely earned the respect of UFC fighters. Whatever art they choose to study to integrate effective kicks into their own arsenal, most UFC fighters keep an eye out for a chance to unleash their own brand of kickboxing on an unwary opponent.

| PRO-FILES | Georges "Rush" St-Pierre |

(Photo courtesy Zuffa, LLC)

Fighting out of: Montreal, Quebec, Canada
Born: 5/19/81
Height: 5'10"
Weight: 170 lbs.
Weightclass: Welterweight
Former UFC Welterweight Champion

Georges started his martial arts training when he was only six years old, and he turned pro in the MMA world in 2002. Now, with an arsenal of Brazilian Jiu-Jitsu, Muay Thai, wrestling, and boxing techniques, Georges stands as one of the best 170-pound fighters in the world and a former UFC Welterweight champ. Known for his amazing athleticism and varied attacks, Georges' most impressive wins are over Matt Hughes (TKO in round two at UFC 65), BJ Penn (split decision at UFC 58), and Sean Sherk (TKO in round two at UFC 56).

Wrestling with It

Like the arts of the Far East that emphasize groundfighting, wrestling is the western world's answer to scuffling on the mat. Stretching back far into the annals of time, wrestling has had a place on the field of combat and organized sports for well over 2,000 years.

UFC fighters who specialize in wrestling today usually have a background in one of the two most popular styles of wrestling. Some of them learned the art back in their high school and college days. Others simply learned by doing it in whatever venue they found themselves.

In any event, wrestling has solidified its place as a valuable asset to UFC fighters. Hall of Famer Dan Severn used his wrestling skills to tremendous advantage during his years as a UFC and MMA fighter, and today fighters such as Randy Couture and Matt Hughes still wave the wrestling flag proudly.

Freestyle Wrestling

One of the oldest forms of grappling in the world, freestyle wrestling uses throws and pins to decide the outcome of a match. Some of the oldest art and sculpture throughout the world shows demonstrations of this art.

Nowadays, freestyle wrestling has an established set of rules and judging criteria. Three officials score the match. A referee controls the action, a chairman on the edge of the mat watches the clock to ensure time restrictions are met, and a judge scores the bout as it unfolds. A majority of the three must consent to points awarded, fouls assessed, or pins called.

There are five ways to win in freestyle wrestling: a fall, a technical fall (based on a six-point lead in scoring), a decision, a disqualification, or an injury. In matches sanctioned by FILA, wrestling's international governing body, Freestyle wrestling uses three two-minute rounds for each bout.

Greco Roman Wrestling

Almost identical to freestyle wrestling, Greco Roman does not allow attacks below the waist. In freestyle wrestling, a fighter attempting to throw his opponent could be thwarted by attacking his legs. In Greco Roman wrestling, using a defensive move like this would be considered illegal. As a result, Greco Roman wrestlers favor throws as a means of gaining victory, and displays of throws in Greco Roman matches sometimes border on the truly spectacular.

Like freestyle wrestling, Greco Roman uses three officials to score the match and control the action. Each bout also uses rounds, but of varying lengths depending on level.

While many fans assert that Greco Roman wrestling derives from the ancient form of combat practiced in Sparta and throughout the Roman Empire, in reality this is false. Spartans and Romans practiced another art known as Pankration, and it was one of the original Olympic sports.

Whatever style of wrestling a UFC fighter may choose to study, the benefits cannot be overstated. Learning how to work into holds and escape from those holds can truly benefit anyone looking to fight in the Octagon.

UFC LEGENDS — **Hall of Famer: Dan "The Beast" Severn**

Fought out of: Coldwater, Michigan
Born: 6/8/54
Height: 6'2"
Weight: 250 lbs.
Weightclass: Heavyweight
UFC 5 Tournament Champion and Superfight Champion

The ever-popular Dan Severn worked his way into the stratosphere of UFC and MMA fighters by capitalizing on his tremendous wrestling skills and his willingness to take on any and all challengers in a variety of bouts all over the world. Still an active competitor in his 50s, Dan remains one of the most visible proponents of MMA and runs a 10,000-square-foot facility on his property in Michigan. Dan's most notable fights include wins over Ken Shamrock, Oleg Taktarov, and Tank Abbott. Dan was inducted into the UFC Hall of Fame in 2005.

Jiu-Jitsu, Jujutsu, Jujitsu

Translated as the "gentle art," real Jiu-Jitsu is anything but gentle. Originating in Japan thousands of years ago, the art encompassed striking, grappling, and ground-fighting techniques. As the martial arts evolved in Japan, numerous families known as "ryuha" established themselves as Jujutsu centers of study.

Gradually, these Jujutsu schools focused less on other forms of combat and began specializing more and more in the grappling techniques that have reached fighters today. As the political and social climate in Japan shifted away from a warrior society, the need for schools that taught combat survival diminished. For more and more Japanese, Jujutsu became something more akin to a hobby than a lifestyle.

In the early twentieth century, as Japan opened to the west, scholars and explorers began experiencing the methods of Jujutsu. They brought these techniques back to the United States and the United Kingdom and other parts of Europe.

Meanwhile, numerous Japanese Jujutsu experts were also traveling all over the world, putting on displays of their prowess. Gradually, the "tricks" of Jujutsu were becoming known.

While there are still plenty of schools in Japan that teach Jujutsu as a complete combat system, most foreign schools have chosen to focus on the grappling aspects of the art. Jujutsu uses joint locks, armbars, throws, choke holds, and other submission techniques to gain a victory over an opponent.

FIGHTER FACTS

The proper spelling of "Jujutsu" has long been a source of confusion for fans and scholars. It's actually fairly simple. Japanese arts are properly spelled "Jujutsu" as directly translated from that language. The term Jiu-Jitsu was used by Mitsuyo Maeda to distinguish his art from Kano's Judo and to account for the Brazilian Portuguese dialects. Jujitsu was the Americanized spelling of the Japanese art, but is rarely used nowadays.

For UFC fighters, techniques from this art are a priceless addition to their repertoire. Jujutsu's more accurate definition and overriding philosophy of "yielding to an opponent's power in order to redirect and thereby gain victory" helps teach today's fighters that going head-to-head is not always the best option. Sometimes, yielding will expose a weakness in their opponent that they may then take advantage of.

Jujutsu also offers fighters other methods of applying takedowns, throws, chokes, submission holds, and counters and escapes.

No matter how it is spelled, Jujutsu, Jiu-Jitsu, or Jujitsu remains a great complement to any fighter's toolbox.

Notable Fights

December 16, 1994: Expo Square Pavilion, Tulsa, Oklahoma

At the culmination of the event's eight-man tournament, Dan Severn faced off against Royce Gracie. Since it was still early on in the UFC's history, there were no time limits, rounds, or judges in the event. It was simply a matter of hanging tough and defeating every comer.

Dan Severn, with his incredible career record as a wrestler, appeared unstoppable in his UFC debut as he won both of his preliminary bouts in a combined 2:37. Severn also outweighed Gracie by approximately 90 pounds, so fans expected that the Brazilian Jiu-Jitsu wizard had finally met his match.

Instead Gracie showed that his style could work, even against a skilled and massive opponent. Severn opened the match by taking Gracie down to the ground, but Gracie quickly assumed the guard position and stayed there.

Severn, intent on winning, pounded Gracie mercilessly through the fight. As time ticked by, Gracie began showing wear from Severn's strikes.

Suddenly, at the fifteen-minute mark, Gracie maneuvered himself into position and caught Severn in a triangle choke that quickly dispatched the larger man. Severn tapped out in defeat at 15:49.

Judo

Also originating in Japan, Judo evolved out of Jujutsu techniques. Professor Jigoro Kano was searching for a fitness regimen that could be implemented in schools across Japan as a means of keeping the nation's youth in good physical condition.

Already a Jujutsu master teacher, Kano took out the more lethal techniques and focused instead on throws, chokes, and submission holds for his new art. He also stressed the need to use an opponent's weight against him. By altering a person's balance and applying the right amount of force, truly awesome throws could be performed. Kano's techniques also empowered smaller fighters to prevail even when dealing with larger opponents.

At the start of the twentieth century, Judo teachers journeyed beyond Japan's shores to demonstrate the effectiveness of the art to nations around the world. As a result, Judo became an Olympic sport and remains immensely popular to this day.

Many UFC fighters study Judo as a means of understanding the dynamics and techniques that are involved in throws and takedowns. Judo's emphasis on such techniques are welcomed by savvy fighters looking to expand their knowledge.

The Least You Need to Know

- Early UFC fights mixed different stylists, but today's fighters mix their techniques to truly embody the concept of MMA.

- Boxing uses hand strikes and footwork to set up opponents for defeat.

- Kickboxing builds on boxing's principles through the use of feet, shins, legs, knees, and even elbows to defeat opponents.

- Wrestling—be it freestyle or Greco Roman—is one of the world's oldest forms of combat and focuses on throws or takedowns, mat control, and pins.

- Jiu-Jitsu (or Jujutsu) originated in Japan and uses joint locks and arm and leg locks, as well as throws and takedowns.

- Judo tends to focus on spectacular throws, submissions, and pins to win its bouts.

5

Styles Make Fights

In This Chapter

- No Two Fighters Alike
- Strengths and Weaknesses: It's All Relative
- Standup Artists
- Ground-and-Pounders
- Submission Specialists

With the amazing variety of martial arts history and fight backgrounds that today's UFC® fighters have, is it any wonder that no two fighters work the Octagon™ the same way? The breadth of experience, strategic inclinations, and even motivational factors all influence how each fighter views his opponents.

Especially interesting is how some fighters who may have backgrounds stemming from arts that are traditionally more of the standup variety may actually prefer fighting on the ground. Or they may have worked to acquire so much skill in an area that was once lacking, that they now are better at that particular discipline than their original "bread and butter" skills.

It's an interesting mix of men who walk into the Octagon ready to do battle. Along with their varied fighting backgrounds, they bring personal lives that span the spectrum of society. And as seemingly nonimportant as those personal lives may be, they, too, have a role in shaping how UFC fighters rise to the challenge of being a new millennium warrior.

In this chapter, we take a close look at how fighters, while trying to expand their repertoires, still inevitably tend to favor what they're most familiar with. The background of basic skills that they may be trying to adapt or morph into something bigger, may in fact be the thing that enables them to win when it's most important: in the Octagon—in front of tens of thousands of screaming fans.

The Individuality of Battle

Let's take a look at some of the current crop of UFC battlers. Each of these men brings something different to the table and even while some of them may appear to have common backgrounds, there is little similarity between them. Each is unique.

UFC Fight Night: Evans and Salmon

In the light heavyweight division, Rashad Evans defeated Sean Salmon in the second round of their fight at UFC Fight Night in January 2007 by delivering a devastating kick to Salmon's head from long range. Evans considers himself very strong in takedowns and takedown defense and was a Division I wrestler at Michigan State University. Yet his athleticism and standup training with trainer Greg Jackson in Albuquerque were clearly evident when he put Salmon down and out with one of the most difficult standup techniques to pull off successfully. So while Salmon may have been looking for a ground fight with Evans, Rashad turned the tables and took his opponent out while the two were standing.

Would it be right to call Evans a striker, then? Definitely not! Evans clearly shows that it is quite possible to combine skills and still remain unique as the fight unfolds. He was facing a fellow wrestler, but decided that his best course of action was to keep his opponent standing because he had a decided edge on the feet against Salmon.

Rashad Evans.

(Photo courtesy Zuffa, LLC)

UFC 62: Gouveia and Combs

Consider also the case of Wilson Gouveia. This light heavyweight has a black belt in Brazilian Jiu-Jitsu but really enjoys peppering his opponents with strikes. In his win, however, against Wes Combs, it wasn't Gouveia's "heavy hands" that won him the fight at UFC 62 in August 2006, it was his ability to force his opponent to submit.

Again, Gouveia has been working on his striking skills, trying to make himself a better all-around fighter. He's been successful with it, too. Experts have noted that his willingness to let punches fly and land them hard should hold him in good stead. But when he needed the win, Gouveia reverted to what he knew he did best: his submission abilities.

UFC 61: Jordan and Franca

Another example of this can be seen in the lightweight division. Hermes Franca used his groundfighting abilities to win out over Joe Jordan on July 8, 2006, at UFC 61. In the third round, Franca finished Jordan with a submission hold. This was despite

Franca's interest in left hooks and elbow strikes. He's been adding to his striking arsenal, but again, when it was time to win the match, he went for the submission and got it, a credit to his experience as a Brazilian Jiu-Jitsu ace.

Hermes Franca.

(Photo courtesy Zuffa, LLC)

Or consider middleweight champion Anderson Silva—known as a ferocious striker, Silva won his first two UFC fights by stirring first-round knockouts. In his third bout against fellow Jiu-Jitsu black belt Travis Lutter at UFC 67 on February 3, 2007, Silva showed his all-around game after being taken down to the ground, as he submitted Lutter with a triangle choke in the second round.

Who's Strong? Who's Weak?

So with all of these incredible fighters out there bashing each other with hands and feet and taking opponents down and submitting them, how easy is it to gauge strengths and weaknesses? Is it possible to stand fighters against each other and make an accurate judgment of ability? Can you predict which fighter will take the day?

On some levels, it's certainly possible to try to predict the outcome before it happens. You can take a look at a fighter's record and see how many times they've won or lost. You can take a look at their past opponents and try to figure out how tough each fight was compared to the upcoming match. And you could certainly look at the supposed strengths of each fighter and reason that if fighter A has good striking ability and his opponent doesn't have a good *chin*, then perhaps fighter A can take the fight if he can land some punches.

But is that all there is to understanding strengths and weaknesses? The easy answer is no. There are tons of factors that come into play any time an expert or fan tries to call a match. Fighters are, after all, human beings with personal lives, bad days, good days, and days when those prized techniques may simply just not feel good.

Still, fans, experts, and especially bookmakers all try. Odds can run long in Vegas, as gamblers pick their favorite thoroughbreds to come out in the end. The following sections explain some of the things they look for when making their picks.

> **FIGHTSPEAK**
>
> Having a good **chin** is a term that hearkens back to the world of boxing. When fighters are said to have a good chin, it means they can take a punch and still fight. Conversely, if someone has a "glass jaw," it means they cannot take very much damage and are liable to fall apart the second a significant punch lands.

Last Man Standing

UFC fighters who like to stay on their feet need two things above all else: excellent striking ability and good takedown defense. By using their strikes—especially solid, fast kicks and punches, they can keep an opponent at bay. Optimally, they can keep the other guy at just the right range for landing those debilitating hits.

At the same time, they need to be able to withstand a sudden charge from their opponent, who might be looking to score a takedown on them.

Fighters who like being upright need to be able to land solid shots. This means a lot of work on heavy bags to condition hands and feet. It means they need to be able to land these power shots on actual opponents and target the strikes to areas that will actually damage their opponent.

Being able to drive a punch into a viable target and quickly bring it back into a good defensive position are also essential. Fighters don't like to leave punches hanging out there. Not only is that weapon not chambered and able to then deliver a lot of power, it also exposes an opening that the opposition may take advantage of.

Chuck Liddell.

(Photo courtesy Zuffa, LLC)

How good are they at pacing? Chuck Liddell is one of the most well-known punchers around. And while he looks for early knockouts, he is also respected for his stamina, having gone into the third and fourth rounds for wins over Tito Ortiz and Jeremy Horn, respectively. Other knockout artists aren't as prepared, and in their zest to get the early KO, they are apt to tire themselves out. A savvy opponent may be able to stay alive just long enough for them to burn out before moving in for a finish.

How standup guys react to takedown attempts can also be critical. If they allow themselves to get taken down, then their entire game may be in jeopardy. A good standup fighter knows how to dismantle a takedown attempt and then use it to his advantage.

But if a standup fighter gets taken down, they need a good defense. Again using Chuck Liddell as an example, if he gets taken down, he is usually able to get right back on his feet again. This is crucial, especially if the fighter in question feels more comfortable on two feet rather than on the ground.

> **PRO-FILES**   **Sean "Muscle Shark" Sherk**
>
> *(Photo courtesy Zuffa, LLC)*
>
> **Fighting out of: Oak Grove, Minnesota**
> **Born: 8/5/73**
> **Height: 5'6"**
> **Weight: 155 lbs.**
> **Weightclass: Lightweight**
> **UFC Lightweight Champion and former welterweight title challenger**
>
> With a strong wrestling background, Sean is one of the best wrestlers competing in the UFC today, but his boxing has rapidly improved over the last couple of years, showing how dangerous he can be in the Octagon. His most recent win at *UFC 64: Unstoppable* on October 14, 2006, over Kenny Florian was a five-round war that proved how much heart and skill Sherk has when tested. After that unanimous decision win over the gutsy Florian, fans and MMA insiders believe Sherk will be in for a long reign atop the 155-pound weight class.

Pounding on the Ground

Other fighters actually look for a way to get to the ground, assume a mount, and then beat the stuffing out of their opponents with heavy-handed strikes. While these fighters can certainly work on the ground, they need several attributes to make the ground their true domain.

Ground-and-pound.

(Photo courtesy Zuffa, LLC)

Like standup fighters, they need to be able to hit and hit hard. Striking while on the ground means that there's less opportunity to generate the same type of power that a standup fighter can generate by coordinating his foot movement with his punches and kicks. Striking while on the ground means a fighter must be able to generate power with his muscle mass more than body movement, since typically his movements are somewhat restricted as he maintains control over his opponent.

A lot of fighters in this category also practice with a heavy bag. But whereas a standup guy would have a heavy bag suspended on chains, the ground striker will usually straddle the heavy bag and practice punching into it that way. Proper exercise—especially with weights and other forms of resistance training—play a crucial role in developing adequate punching power for these fighters.

Ground strikers also need excellent ground defense work. Obviously, as they're raining down punches, their opponents will be looking for ways to escape the mount, reverse the position, and administer their own striking storm. Fighters in this category must be acutely aware of their opponent's position as the fight continues—alert to any possible counters before the opponent can unleash them.

UFC LEGENDS — **Oleg "The Russian Bear" Taktarov**

(Photo courtesy Zuffa, LLC)

Born: 6/25/68
Height: 6'0"
Weight: 210 lbs.
Weightclass: Heavyweight
UFC 6 Tournament Winner

A practitioner of the Russian art of Sambo and Japanese Judo, Taktarov made his name during the early years of the UFC, fighting other UFC notables like Tank Abbott and Dan Severn. Taktarov trained with Ken Shamrock for a time and eventually faced him in the UFC. The two fighters fought to a standstill, and in 1998, Taktarov retired from mixed martial arts competition to work on his acting. Since then, he has appeared in several films and released several instructional videotapes. Taktarov is best known for his calm demeanor, unorthodox takedowns, and for one of the bloodiest fights in UFC's history against Dan Severn in UFC 5.

Submitted for Your Approval

For wrestlers, Jiu-Jitsu exponents, or fighters who just love working on the ground, they need a ready menu of skills they can call on to make the fight theirs.

Fighters in this category need to be able to get to the ground safely, with their opponent, prior to submitting them. For this to happen, they need to be able to take their opponents down. Standup fighters and ground strikers will naturally be looking for openings as the submission expert moves in. A standup striker will try to decipher the range between them and nail them with a kick or punch as they come in. A ground striker might let himself be taken down, provided he ends up in a dominant position that allows him to then unleash hell.

FIGHTER FACTS

Bear in mind that a fighter doesn't necessarily have to be on the ground in order to get a submission. There are submission techniques that can be applied standing up. The general flow of a fight in the Octagon, however, usually means that almost all of the submissions in the cage take place on the ground.

A submission in action.

(Photo courtesy Zuffa, LLC)

The submission expert's job, then, is to take his opponent down without walking into a punch or kick. He has to be able to protect himself during the takedown, aware that the ground striker will be looking for that mount position once they hit the floor.

Once on the floor, the submission fighter needs to be able to work his opponent into a choke or submission hold, keenly aware that he may be facing counter strikes or counter holds. Sweat makes the skin slippery and adds a dimension of difficulty to the fight. Pacing is also critical since groundfighting can rapidly exhaust even a seasoned veteran.

Lastly, the submission expert must know how to apply his holds without fail. If his opponent knows how to counter those holds, the submission fighter should know the counter to the counter and so on.

Notable Fights

(Photo courtesy Zuffa, LLC)

February 5, 2005: Mandalay Bay Arena, Las Vegas, Nevada

In what was viewed as a chance for Tito Ortiz, the "Huntington Beach Bad Boy," to reclaim his position as an elite fighter in the UFC, following losses to Randy Couture and Chuck Liddell, *UFC 51: Super Saturday* delivered all the excitement it promised.

In his second comeback fight, Ortiz faced off against Brazilian bomber Vitor "The Phenom" Belfort, a fighter once known for his explosive striking attacks, but who could also hold his own on the mat. Belfort looked set to take Ortiz out early on in the match with a giant left hand that left Ortiz bleeding and shaken. But Ortiz, to his credit, withstood the assault and even scored with a few strikes of his own toward the end of round one.

In round two, Belfort again started strong as he rapidly got Ortiz in a guillotine choke. Ortiz managed to escape the lock but as he did so, Belfort punished him with a series of hard elbows. When the two fighters were put back on their feet, however, Ortiz seemed to snap back to his old self, getting a quick takedown and then unleashing his own barrage of elbows to Belfort.

In the third round, the old Ortiz that the fans wanted to see was back. After getting another takedown, he unleashed his own ground-and-pound devastation, repeatedly striking Belfort until the end of the round.

A split decision by the judges followed the match, but at the end, Ortiz was the winner and was back on his way up the light heavyweight ladder.

While fighters may find themselves typecast into certain categories by fans or by virtue of the techniques they themselves favor, it's important to note that every category has its own inherent strengths and weaknesses. As we've seen, a standup fighter may be vulnerable to takedowns if his defense isn't good. A ground striker may find himself countered and suddenly caught in a choke hold if he is not alert to such things. And a submission fighter may walk right into a left roundhouse kick to the head on his way to trying a takedown.

Today's UFC fighters try to ensure their own success by limiting those weaknesses by cross-training in other styles. By doing so, they minimize their chances of losing a match.

The gap between success and failure gets narrower with every new technique learned, with every new opponent overcome, and with every new experience.

The Least You Need to Know

- ◆ UFC fighters today are not carbon copies, but unique individuals who all bring something different to the sport.

- ◆ Strengths and weaknesses of each fighter are gauged by past experience, skill, and many other intangibles.

- ◆ Standup fighters need excellent striking skills and solid takedown defense in order to shine.

- ◆ Ground strikers need to deliver heavy hits while maintaining control over their opponent.

- ◆ Submission fighters must protect themselves during the takedown and get their holds on fast and tight.

Chapter 6

Fight Strategy 101

In This Chapter

- ◆ Advantage Striking
- ◆ Advantage Wrestling
- ◆ Advantage Submissions

We've seen the variety of ways that UFC® fighters work to impose their dominance in the Octagon™ based on their past training and experiences. Some of the fighters work at a distance, striking their opponents and looking for knockouts. Others prefer to get a takedown and pound their opponents on the ground, while still others maneuver to get their opponent into a submission hold.

Based on what their strengths and weaknesses might be, fighters try to develop strategies to maximize their strengths and limit their liabilities. Each one views the unfolding fight in a different way. As a result, their strategies then become as individual as the fighters themselves.

In this chapter, we take a look at how each category carries within it inherent advantages that, properly applied, can be the difference between victory and defeat.

The Upside of Striking

The first immediate advantage that strikers have in the Octagon is how the fight itself starts. Both competitors are stood up, facing each other across the ring. This is standup striking territory, and for those fighters who like to operate here this immediately puts them in a favorable position. The distance is such that they can rapidly bring their long-range weapons into play.

Consider a fighter who looks to feel his opponent out with a series of punches. A simple boxer's jab can cause a reaction in the opponent that opens him up for a roundhouse kick to the head. Or he may try to slip the jab, in which case the standup striker may nail him with an overhand right.

Any one of these strikes can lead to a knockout, and it's something that standup strikers are constantly looking for. The more dramatic the knockout, the better. And the search for such amazing displays of striking power has led to fighters being labeled *headhunters*.

(Photo courtesy Zuffa, LLC)

Headhunting is a term used to denote fighters who like going after spectacular knockout shots—usually by strictly attacking the heads of their opponents with huge punches or kicks and ignoring body punching. Obviously, if the attack is successful, it's a great piece of work. But being overzealous about going after knockouts can also leave the standup fighter prone to counter attacks. As with everything else, there are positives and negatives associated with each type of strategy.

The Rock

Pedro "The Rock" Rizzo is a great example of someone who, during his UFC career, always looked for a chance to score the huge hit that would get him a knockout. The four-time Brazilian Muay Thai champion has an incredible record outside of the UFC as well, with 30 of his 31 reported kickboxing victories coming by way of knockout.

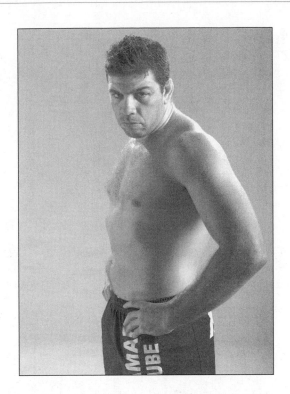

Pedro Rizzo.

(Photo courtesy Zuffa, LLC)

Rizzo put his arsenal of amazing kicks and punches to use in the Octagon to great effect, winning bouts over Andrei Arlovski, Josh Barnett, Tra Telligman, and Tank Abbott. Rizzo worked to use his strikes during the standup portions of a fight, when he knew they would be most effective and best positioned.

Although Rizzo left the UFC in 2003, his ability to use his kicks and punches to great advantage while standing is certainly worthy of examination. Rizzo's greatest liability, as it was noted by UFC fight commentator Joe Rogan, wasn't his lack of ability, it was his lackadaisical attitude. His lack of an aggressive killer instinct hurt him in his quest for the UFC heavyweight title.

The Saint and Body-Slamming Hughes

Georges St-Pierre is another fighter who likes looking for the finishing blow that will give him the knockout. Consider his match against Matt Hughes at UFC 65. In the first round, St-Pierre opened with a series of kicks looking to establish the proper distance for his striking ability. As they sometimes do in traditional boxing, St-Pierre also used his jab effectively, setting Hughes up for follow-up kicks. When the two fighters went to the ground after St-Pierre scored with a "Superman punch," the Canadian standout continued to use his striking effectively, hurting Hughes just as the round ended.

Georges St-Pierre.

(Photo courtesy Zuffa, LLC)

In round two, St-Pierre opened with a lead jab that set up a brutal head kick. Working the distance that enabled him to strike most effectively, St-Pierre won the championship from Hughes. He used strikes that worked best at long range and then as he moved in closer, switched to close-in elbow strikes to demolish Hughes. Clearly, St-Pierre knows how to work the distance in conjunction with effective strikes to maximize his chances of a spectacular knockout.

In this case, a fighter who knows how to use distancing, and who sets his shots up well (a la the jab to set up a kick) can dismantle his opponents.

But what about strikers who enjoy the ground-and-pound strategy of taking their opponents down before unleashing their shots? Despite his loss to Georges St-Pierre at UFC 65, Matt Hughes has consistently shown his ability to take his opponents down with some really amazing slams. These are a lot of fun to watch from the spectator standpoint, and are also a key piece of Hughes's strategy.

A takedown.

(Photo courtesy Zuffa, LLC)

By slamming his opponents to the ground, Hughes sets them up for the next part of the equation, namely, the pound. As his opponents are struggling to recover from getting slammed to the mat, Hughes is already working his way into the mount, and readying his elbow strikes or close-in punches that have earned him knockouts in the past.

Hughes has also tailored his own training to include more striking work in order to complement his ground-and-pound strategy. Obviously, this strategy can backfire, as St-Pierre so effectively demonstrated when Hughes wasn't able to protect himself very well during the standup and was unable to secure a takedown.

On the flip side, St-Pierre could have easily found himself on the wrong side of Hughes's strategy if St. Pierre hadn't worked on achieving a good takedown defense.

Ground-and-Pound Randy

Randy Couture is another UFC champion who has earned a number of wins from his own ground-and-pound. Couture has a fair standup game, yes, but knows his strengths lie in getting his opponents down to the mat where he can then unleash his strikes. A wrestler by nature, Couture has amended his game by adding some devastating ground strikes and a serviceable standup attack to his arsenal.

Randy Couture.

(Photo courtesy Zuffa, LLC)

Standup strikers have the advantage of being able to hit hard and potentially end fights before they begin. If a standup fighter has poor takedown defense, then the grappler enjoys the advantage of being able to take him down and then set about punishing him.

Life on the Mat

Some of the UFC's most recognizable names have a deep background in wrestling. What is it about this sport that adds such a vital dimension to UFC fighters? Where does the advantage lie in being well-versed in wrestling?

Wrestlers are extremely adept at takedowns and then maneuvering to work ground and pound attacks on their opponents. A wrestler's strength lies in his ability to keep his opponents back on the mat and control him while search for openings to strike.

In a clinch, a wrestler can score dramatic takedowns or slams that set up their opponent for a submission hold or a ground-and-pound onslaught. Many wrestlers have also added striking to their repertoire, seeking to expand upon their natural love of the mat.

Wrestling: Josh Koscheck

One of the UFC's rising stars who acknowledges his preference for wrestling is Josh Koscheck. Koscheck, who has only been fighting professionally since 2004, has scored two impressive first-round wins over Jonathan Goulet and Ansar Chalangov, and decisioned highly regarded Diego Sanchez.

Josh Koscheck goes for the takedown against Jeff Joslin.

(Photo courtesy Zuffa, LLC)

Koscheck used a series of successive takedowns to soften up opponent Jeff Joslin at UFC Fight Night 7 in December 2006. Eventually winning by unanimous decision, Koscheck seems poised to fully implement the advantages he has found in his wrestling acumen.

Wrestling: Sean Sherk

Sean Sherk is another UFC fighter who favors the wrestling advantage. Sherk's most recent win over Kenny Florian showed that wrestlers enjoy the advantage of being extremely comfortable working on the ground. During the standup portion of the fight, Sherk closed the gap, always going for the takedown by either latching on for control or by covering his efforts with strikes.

Another key advantage is the ability to pace a fight and go the distance. Sherk needed that endurance in order to ensure his victory over Florian during the match in October 2006. Unlike a lot of strikers, wrestlers often have a measure of endurance that lets them win out over fighters not as well conditioned due to their focus on anaerobic as opposed to aerobic activity.

Sean Sherk.

(Photo courtesy Zuffa, LLC)

Comfort on the mat, pacing, and the ability to acquire and escape from holds gives fighters who favor wrestling strategies some impressive advantages. They must be careful while trying to impose their will, however. A skilled striker with a good take-down defense can rattle them as they attempt their tactics.

The Submission Advantage

It's been said that there's nothing more dangerous on the ground than a submission specialist who knows his stuff. UFC fighters who like working on submissions go after some excruciating holds and chokes that many fans like watching nearly as much as spectacular knockout strikes.

The task for a submission specialist is to get his opponent on the ground in such a way that he doesn't get punished for doing so. Many submission fighters work on their standup game just enough to be able to withstand some of the shots necessary to get the fight on the ground.

(Photo courtesy Zuffa, LLC)

Fighting out of: San Jose, California
Born: 6/19/79
Height: 6'1"
Weight: 185 lbs.
Weightclass: Middleweight
Top middleweight contender, member of the first season cast of *The Ultimate Fighter®.*

Known for his striking, speed, and aggression, this up-and-comer is one of the stars of *The Ultimate Fighter®* who has made his way into the Octagon in impressive fashion. Scoring two first-round submission wins against Steve Vigneault and Joe Riggs at UFC 58 and UFC 60, respectively, Mike established himself as a versatile fighter intent on making his mark in the sport. His biggest win to date came via unanimous decision against David Loiseau at UFC 63. Mike's background in Tae Kwon Do, kickboxing, and Muay Thai, along with his training in Brazilian Jiu-Jitsu, have helped round him out as a fighter definitely worth watching.

It's dangerous, but the payoff can be immense.

Consider the events of UFC 52, when Ivan Salaverry asserted himself over Joe Riggs in the very first round of their match. Salaverry won the match, rapidly trapping Riggs in a triangle choke that sealed the deal. Prior to gaining the choke, Salaverry seemed content to let Riggs suggest the flow of the fight. But Salaverry had a game plan and he knew that if Riggs felt he was in control, he might just expose himself. Salaverry was right and when Riggs gave him the moment, Salaverry took control.

Submission fighters know an endless variety of chokes and locks that they use to great advantage over other fighters. In the course of a standup segment, for example, a kick that stays out too long can be snagged and used for a takedown.

During the clinch, a submission fighter can position himself to exploit openings. And whereas a wrestler might be looking for a great throw or takedown, the submission fighter may use that to secure the wrestler in a vicious armlock.

A submission fighter may also endure a choke or lock for longer than a fighter less well-versed in them. Submission fighters also practice escapes from the very holds they look to use, giving them the added advantage over other fighters if they find themselves on the wrong side of a choke.

Salaverry and Riggs battle it out at UFC 52.

(Photo courtesy Zuffa, LLC)

UFC LEGENDS — David "Tank" Abbott

(Photo courtesy Zuffa, LLC)

Fought out of: Huntington Beach, California
Born: 4/26/65
Height: 6'0"
Weight: 250 lbs.
Weightclass: Heavyweight

Despite the fact that Tank never succeeded in securing a championship title in the UFC, there's little doubt that he remains one of MMA's fan favorites. With a style that he honed through boxing and wrestling in Huntington Beach, Tank won fans over with his sheer aggression and power—as well as a healthy dose of controversial comments and behavior. Often portrayed as a bad boy in the media, Tank remains an endearing figure to fans in the world of mixed martial arts and combat sports.

Notable Fights

(Photo courtesy Zuffa, LLC)

August 21, 2004: MGM Grand Garden Arena, Las Vegas, Nevada

A spectacular display of ground-and-pounding at its best, this matchup in the light heavyweight division saw Randy Couture face off against Vitor Belfort for the third time in front of a packed house at the MGM Grand in Las Vegas.

During round one, it seemed that both fighters were feeling each other out, although Couture seemed infinitely more relaxed than his opponent. Toward the end of the round, Couture gets a takedown on Belfort and starts what would become the trend for the entire fight by ground-and-pounding him against the cage.

Early in round two, it appears that Belfort has suffered a laceration above his eye as a result of a bashing of heads. Couture seizes on the cut, unleashing a startling volley of shots when he repeatedly takes Belfort to the mat. At the 1:32 mark, referee John McCarthy asks for a doctor to check on Belfort's cut, which Couture has successfully turned into a massive gash. The doctor gives the okay for the fight to continue, but there's no question that the end is near.

In round three, Belfort attempts to secure an armbar on Couture, but there's simply no chance of success. Couture takes Belfort down to the mat again and resumes his ground-and-pound attack, suffocating Belfort with a barrage of punches and elbows.

At the end of a bloody round three, the fight is stopped and Couture pronounced the winner. He is once again the UFC light heavyweight champion.

If anything, with each specialty having its own advantages over other specialties, UFC fighters today need a wide array of techniques in order to survive inside the Octagon.

It's simply not enough to be proficient in just one discipline. A striker needs to know submissions and how to work on the ground. A wrestler needs to know how to strike and submit. A submission fighter needs to know how to strike and wrestle.

With more and more fighters coming into mixed martial arts than ever before—especially as the UFC gains the prominence it deserves—the need for a fighter to be well grounded and capable of capitalizing on any opportunity is paramount. Not being able to work in all areas of combat sports means that a career may be over before it's even begun. Understanding the advantages and disadvantages of each portion of a fight can spell the difference between a great fighter and a wannabe.

The Least You Need to Know

♦ Strikers use a combination of proper distance with punches and kicks to impose their will.

♦ Wrestlers use a variety of moves to take their opponents down and then get the win.

♦ Submission specialists look for locks and chokes to take their opponents out.

Part 3

"As Real As It Gets"®

Ready to step inside the Octagon™? In this part, we look at the three stages of a fight: the standup, the clinch, and the shoot for the takedown. Each part has its own weapons and strategies, and we take a close look at each, including some unique things UFC® fighters do to give them an edge.

Keeping the Fight Standing

In This Chapter

- ◆ A Look at Footwork
- ◆ Timing and Distancing
- ◆ Punching Combinations
- ◆ Punching/Kicking Combinations
- ◆ Defending the Takedown

Generally speaking, there are three distinct phases of any fight in the Octagon™. As each fight progresses, it's a fair bet that fans will see situations involving all three.

Fighters in the UFC® always start standing up, coming at each other from across the Octagon. Once they are close to striking distance, blows may be exchanged. The fighters may then move to the second stage of combat, the clinch, or immediately go for a takedown to get the fight to the third stage, the battle on the ground.

In this chapter, we take a look at how fighters work to keep the battle standing. At this stage, fighters with excellent striking skills enjoy a greater advantage and are able to bring the full brunt of their arsenals to bear on their opponents. As they look to score a knockout, they also will be watching to guard against their opponent closing the distance. Staying upright can be a definite challenge.

Fancy Feet

In order to deliver effective strikes, fighters use several basic principles to impart the maximum force. By doing so, they hope to score those all-impressive knockouts.

Footwork is one of the single most important attributes all good UFC fighters seek to cultivate. Without proper, balanced footwork, punches and kicks will lack power. In addition, improperly aligned feet will send strikes off target; a knockout blow becomes a grazing bruise instead. A devastating kick misses its mark entirely.

Fighters must learn to move around the Octagon using footwork that brings them into striking distance, keeps them in good balance as they strike, and maintains a degree of protection as they do so. In other words, as the fighters throw strikes, their bodies are as protected as they can be by virtue of where their feet are positioned.

Setting Up the Punch

Let's take a look at how some UFC fighters use their footwork to set up devastating punches. In the following photos, we examine exactly what's happening.

Liddell vs. Sobral, UFC 62.

(Photo courtesy Zuffa, LLC)

Notice how Chuck Liddell (wearing the Mohawk in the first photo) throws a great left punch directly into Renato Sobral during UFC 62. Liddell's punch is delivered only after his footwork has set it up. Liddell's left foot is forward and aimed directly at Sobral's centerline. Liddell also is leaning into his punch, keeping his knees bent and forward, thereby allowing him to deliver maximum punch force. The effect is rather obvious. Sobral is rocked back from the force of the blow. If Liddell's punch was a few inches higher and had landed on the point of Sobral's chin, there's a good chance Liddell gets himself a knockout. As it was, Liddell got his victory later on in the fight.

Griffin vs. Bonnar, UFC 62.

(Photo courtesy Zuffa, LLC)

Here's another great example of footwork in action. In this photograph, both fighters are positioning themselves for hard punches. Unfortunately, one of them lands his punch first. Forrest Griffin (above on the right side) has set up his overhand right punch to land using great alignment based on his footwork. His left foot is planted and his right foot is up to give him just a bit more reach and power in his punch. He catches Stephan Bonnar perfectly on the side of his chin, delivering a great hit.

For his part, Bonnar is turned, possibly trying to position himself to execute a left hook to the right side of Griffin's head. His right foot is planted just a bit too far away from Griffin. As a result, his hook will miss Griffin's head. If Bonnar had planted his right foot a bit closer—a move that would have also improved his balance—there's a chance he would have made impact. However, fighters do not survive on position alone and in this action sequence, Griffin has the advantage of timing as well, enabling him to land his punch first.

Hominick vs. Edwards, UFC 58.

(Photo courtesy Zuffa, LLC)

Mark Hominick (in white shorts above) uses his footwork to establish a superior position over Yves Edwards at UFC 58 and to deliver a great left punch. Notice how Hominick has aimed his entire body, not just the punch, at the spot he wants to hit. The coordination of body power adds tremendous power to his shots. An additional benefit of his positioning in the photograph is that once he lands that left, he is in great position to come over Edwards's guard and deliver a right cross. Hominick actually goes on to win this bout using a submission, but his punches certainly helped set up the win.

Setting Up the Kick

Like punches, good footwork also establishes a great base for launching superior kicks. Take a look through the following pictures and notice how these fighters use solid footwork to drive their point home—using kicks.

Josh Schockman (in black shorts in the following photo) at *UFC 65: Bad Intentions*, throws a great roundhouse kick at opponent Jake O'Brien's head. Schockman has a solid base on his right leg, with his foot turned out so his left kick can arc up and in at the target. If O'Brien's right hand was not protecting his head, this kick looks like it would certainly have scored a knockout. While Schockman fails to take O'Brien out of the match, this kick is a good example of using footwork to effectively launch strikes like this.

Schockman vs. O'Brien, UFC 65.

(Photo courtesy Zuffa, LLC)

FIGHTER FACTS

With the prevalence of Muay Thai exponents in the UFC, most of the fighters kick with the idea of using their shins to make impact. Kickers may also use the heel, in rare instances such as the occasional side kick or to kick the body of a downed opponent.

By kicking with their shins, fighters also minimize the distance an opponent will have available to counter their kicks.

Hardonk vs. Pendergarst, UFC 65.

(Photo courtesy Zuffa, LLC)

Unlike Schockman in the previous example, Antoni Hardonk (black shorts with white lettering) uses proper footwork to set up a devastating kick to Sherman Pendergarst's left side in UFC 65, scoring him a first-round technical knockout. Hardonk's left foot is turned and planted while his right leg delivers the punishing blow to Pendergarst. Hardonk, formerly a professional Dutch kickboxer and instructor, obviously knows the value of using footwork to set up his kicks.

St-Pierre vs. Hughes, UFC 65.

(Photo courtesy Zuffa, LLC)

And last but not least, here's an example of footwork setting up a tremendous side kick from Georges St-Pierre (foreground above) into Matt Hughes at UFC 65. Hughes has his left arm extended, almost as if he intended to punch St-Pierre, but he is out of range. St-Pierre, however, is in perfect range to land his thunderous side kick. The power of the kick is evident, clearly rocking Hughes back. St-Pierre, by comparison, is in perfect balance and his supporting leg is bent, enabling him to maintain his balance even during the chaos of a fight.

Fighters use a variety of drills to help them achieve good footwork. Skipping rope, running, shadowboxing, sparring, and mirror work all allow a fighter to see how their body moves when they throw strikes. They learn how to move their feet in order to set up powerful combinations that hopefully will garner them knockouts.

The training is necessary to their success. And it helps lay the foundation for fighters as they work on their timing and distancing.

Timing and Distancing

Timing is the ability to hit a target at the right moment to deliver the maximum amount of force behind a strike. Today's UFC fighters understand that a good sense of timing can easily mean the difference between victory and defeat. They train to enhance their sense of timing using a variety of methods.

One of the easiest ways to work on timing is through the use of a speed bag. Boxers have long used this method to work on their punches. The speed bag hangs on a ball joint platform that enables the bag to rotate 360 degrees. Fighters then work on delivering rapid punches to the bag, perfecting a sense of rhythm. More challenging than the speed bag is the double-end striking bag. This free-hanging bag uses a rope at one end and a length of elastic at the other. One part hangs from a fixed point on a ceiling or beam and the other end is weighted at the ground. The ball target itself can be adjusted for head height or body shots. Once the first punch hits the bag, the elastic cord makes it respond unpredictably. Fighters can then work on their reaction to the bag coming back at them and on their timing as they continue to hit it.

The double-end striking bag also helps fighters work on their sense of distancing. The elastic cord enables the bag to move so it is not always in range for a hit. Fighters have to time their punches or kicks to when the bag comes into range.

Fighters today also use training partners to work on both their timing and distancing. In many ways the two are connected, because if a fighter's timing is off, the distance will not necessarily be optimal. Fighters use focus mitts to help them work on both. The options for using focus mitts are endless.

Anyone can hold a set of focus mitts, but it takes a real pro to know how to use them for the fighter's maximum benefit. A good trainer will call out jabs in a random order as well as preset combinations. As he does this, the trainer moves in the same way an opponent would in the Octagon. Occasionally, the trainer will also throw "punches" back at the fighter, forcing the person he is training to react to the attacks by slipping, covering, or countering. The sad truth is that most people who think they know how to hold focus mitts don't do it properly. A UFC fighter needs a trainer who actually knows how to use them as they were intended to be used.

Focus mitts help fighters improve their speed and accuracy. As such, the use of focus mitts is an important component of any training regimen.

Some fighters like to work on the heavy bag as well. As the bag bounces on its chains, the fighters practice punches and kicks, trying to catch the bag during the right point as it swings. In the fight, the development of these skills could easily mean a knockout kick. Without working on these skills, fighters may find all of their strikes failing to connect with their targets.

Using a heavy bag is a key method of learning how to build power in a fighter's strikes. Repeated sessions on a heavy bag help fighters impart maximum force behind their strikes.

Sparring is another way fighters work on improving their game. There's no substitute for training with a live partner who can hit back. During training, fighters may go into a training session with a goal in mind—work on an inside combination or work on long-range kicks. Or they may simply want the challenge of freestyle sparring.

Whatever fighters choose to work on, their timing or distancing, they do so knowing the skills are vital to their development as warriors.

Bridging the Gap

Being able to deliver well-timed kicks and punches has another benefit aside from scoring hits. Punches and kicks can be used to bridge the gap or close the distance between the fighters.

One of the most common ways fighters in the UFC use punches to close the gap is through the use of a jab. A jab is a quick, straight punch thrown with the lead hand from the guard position. Once the jab extends, the fighter will come in behind it, shuffling forward as they do so, thereby paring down the distance.

There is a difference in how some fighters will jab in the UFC compared to boxing. UFC fighters need to be aware of the possibility of their opponent shooting in. If a fighter is facing a striker, his jab may look different from how he jabs a grappler.

In the following photos, notice how Rich Franklin throws a fairly standard jab in the first picture against a striker. But in the second photograph, Rich's body is back a bit, making it harder for his grappling opponent to shoot in on him.

Rich Franklin jabs at a striker.

(Photo courtesy Mickey Suttiratana)

Rich Franklin jabs at a grappler.

(Photo courtesy Mickey Suttiratana)

Fighters also have used crosses to accomplish the same task. Usually the cross is set up with a solid jab that may or may not impact on the opponent. The goal is to set the opponent up in such a way that the cross can be employed, simultaneously bringing the fighter closer to him.

Most UFC fighters prefer to use punches to close the gap. Kicks, because of the fact that the legs are longer, take more time to reach the target. If a fighter chooses to use kicks to bridge the gap, he must fill the extra time with punches as a set-up for the kick. Otherwise, the kick will never be effective. Sometimes the set-up can be accomplished with footwork.

Knowing how to use timing and distancing to their maximum advantage can truly bump a fighter's game up to the next level. There are many examples of fighters working the Octagon these days who know how to time their hits in such a way that they achieve startling results every time.

PRO-FILES — **Rising Star: Keith "The Dean of Mean" Jardine**

(Photo courtesy Zuffa, LLC)

Fighting out of: Albequerque, New Mexico
Born: 10/31/75
Height: 6'2"
Weight: 205 lbs.
Weightclass: Light Heavyweight
Member of *The Ultimate Fighter*® season two cast; highly regarded light heavyweight contender.

To say Keith's resumé bounces around like a pinball wouldn't be unfair. This former personal trainer, firefighter, football coach, and bounty hunter has brought his incredibly well-rounded fight game to the Octagon in spectacular fashion. With his win over Forrest Griffin by technical knockout in the first round at UFC 66, Keith's devotion to the sport will no doubt keep him grounded firmly in the winner's circle for years to come.

Punching Combinations

While every fighter hopes for that one truly awesome punch or kick that will end the fight, the reality is that one-punch or one-kick knockouts are rare—more often since UFC fighters wear much smaller gloves than their boxing counterparts. Fighters therefore work to develop combinations of strikes that will overwhelm their opponent and achieve victory.

Using the jab as the lead part of a combination, fighters know they really only have four basic punches at their disposal: jab, cross, hook, and uppercut. While jabs are great punches and may well score hits, they are also quite effective at staging combinations. But victory often comes down to who puts together the best combination of punches with the best timing.

Here are some of the more popular combinations used in the world of mixed martial arts today.

Jab & Cross

The most basic combination and one of the most effective, the jab/cross works because of how the jab sets the opponent up. Despite the fact that the jab itself may not be the most powerful punch in a fighter's arsenal, multiple jabs can set up a cross or a kick, which can then lead to victory. As the fighter throws the jab, the opponent's reaction is key to how well the cross will work.

When a fighter slips a jab, he tends to do so to the outside of the punch, so the cross is more difficult to reach him. At the same time the fighter slips to the outside of the punch, he will also try to angle. The angle is in the footwork and is important in counter punching and avoiding the next punch of the attack as well. With the angle comes one of two movements: closing movement toward the opponent, closing the distance … possibly looking for a takedown or just jamming him to avoid any subsequent punches being thrown, or with the angle, the fighter can use his footwork to move away to completely avoid the subsequent punches thrown.

The cross punch also has the ability to impart more force than the jab, so the effect is much greater than that of the jab alone.

Jab/Cross/Hook

Building off of the basic jab/cross combination, fighters will add a hook punch to the equation. The hook is a great finisher, set up by the jab/cross combination for the knockout provided everything else has gone well.

Whether or not the cross lands successfully, the opponent may be rocking back and away. At this point, the fighter can follow up with a lead hook, sometimes catching the opponent off of his slip. Rear hooks are generally not thrown since it creates an off-balance stance. Also, if the cross does not come in straight, it may appear to be a hook, when, in fact, it is more of a loop.

If the cross does land, and if the fighter chooses not to employ a lead hook, he has the option of following up with a rear hand cross, looping overhand cross, or possibly an uppercut.

The benefit of using the opposite hand is that it has been set up by the cross and the natural movement of the fighter's body has staged it for maximum power.

On the other hand (literally) by doubling up, the fighter may catch his opponent unaware. If the opponent has dodged the cross and expects the hook from the other side, the double-up may catch him unaware.

*Randy Couture (left) delivers
a thundering cross to Chuck
Liddell during UFC 57.*

(Photo courtesy Zuffa, LLC)

Jab & Uppercut

This combination can be very effective, especially if an opponent has slipped in the same direction several times while avoiding a cross or possible cross. By doing so, he has placed his head in a position whereby the fighter can land the uppercut. The fighter has used the jab or jab/cross combination in this instance several times to set the opponent up for the uppercut.

*Rich Franklin (left) looks to
deliver a brutal uppercut to
Evan Tanner at UFC 52.*

(Photo courtesy Zuffa, LLC)

Jab/Cross/Hook/Uppercut

A series of four punches in rapid succession can be a difficult thing to pull off, even for the most skilled of fighters, but if things are going well, then this combination can easily result in a knockout.

Any time a fighter employs a series of hits, he must constantly move his own body in relation to his opponent's body in order to maintain the proper distance and timing.

The key to punch combinations is that each punch sets up the next punch in the combination. By studying how their bodies deliver certain punches and hits, fighters have the ability to build spectacular combinations that can take an opponent out. They must also realize, however, that while they are trying to deliver their barrage, their opponent will be looking for ways to defend and counter strike. Only through repeated training can fighters hope to learn what combinations will work for them as opposed to what will not.

Combinations therefore are never pre-thought in a fight. Fighters normally begin with a jab (usually thrown with the left hand) and follow up with a right hand strike. The secondary punch depends on how the opponent reacts, and is generally a natural instinct of the fighter throwing it due to the extensive training. After the right hand strike, the fighter usually employs the left hand again. Once again, the punch used will depend on how the opponent has reacted. The process thus continues ...

Combining Hands and Feet

The beauty of punching combinations is that they can be combined with kicks to achieve spectacular knockouts if all factors are favorable. By combining the benefits of kicks and punches, UFC fighters can hammer their opponents in a variety of ways from a variety of distances.

Prior to embarking on the quest for such combinations, however, fighters routinely train themselves on the basics of using individual strikes. Learning how each punch or kick works is the basis for combining them later.

Some of the more common punch/kick combinations follow.

Jab & Roundhouse

Using the jab once again to set up the opponent, many fighters like the reaction it gets. If the opponent raises or lower his hands to deal with the jab, they have opened themselves up for a roundhouse kick. Likewise, if the opponent steps back to avoid the jab, they place themselves at the optimal distance for a roundhouse kick. Evading to one side or the other of the jab places them in a bad position. The momentum generated by the lead jab coupled with the arcing roundhouse kick can be incredible, and the head is a common target for this combination. Also, how the opponent moves—on a linear line or in a circular fashion—will help the fighter decide how to unleash the kick.

Yushin Okami (right) lands a right jab on Rory Singer at UFC 66 …

(Photo courtesy Zuffa, LLC)

… that sets up a perfect left roundhouse kick.

(Photo courtesy Zuffa, LLC)

UFC LEGENDS **Randy Couture**

(Photo courtesy Zuffa, LLC)

Fought out of: Las Vegas, Nevada
Born: 6/22/63
Height: 6'2"
Weight: 220 lbs.
Weightclass: Heavyweight (also competed at light heavyweight)
Three-time UFC Heavyweight and two-time Light Heavyweight Champion

Perhaps the most accomplished fighter to ever compete in the UFC, Randy Couture has thrilled fans for years with his spectacular wrestling ability, underrated striking, and warrior's heart. The only man in UFC history to win the heavyweight title three times and the light heavyweight title twice, Couture left the heavyweight division in 2003 and reinvented himself as a light heavyweight, defeating the likes of Chuck Liddell, Tito Ortiz, and Vitor Belfort to establish himself not only as a 205-pound champion, but as one of the greatest fighters ever to lace up the gloves. Couture was inducted into the UFC Hall of Fame in 2006 and seamlessly entered the UFC broadcast booth as a color commentator. He put his microphone and headset to the side on March 3, 2007, though, when he returned to the heavyweight division to meet and defeat UFC champion Tim Sylvia at UFC 68.

Jab, Cross, Roundhouse

Building yet again on the basics, the jab/cross/roundhouse is a dynamic series that sets the opponent up repeatedly in the hope that he will not be able to keep up with the attack and that one of the blows will score.

The fighter begins with the lead jab and follows with the cross. As the opponent backs away or otherwise evades the cross, the fighter launches the lead leg roundhouse kick. One of the benefits of this combination is the way the roundhouse kick is logically readied once the cross is thrown. The fighter extends the cross, which twists his body and generates a dynamic flex. The roundhouse kick, when launched, carries a great deal of force behind it

Much like we stated above, whichever hand throws the last punch, usually the opposite leg will kick. A right cross will generate the torque (twist in the body) necessary to throw a balanced and powerful roundhouse (or sometimes referred to as a "switch kick").

In the event that any one of the hits in a combination lands, the fighter can simply build on the damage by unleashing the next hits in the series. As such, combinations—whether they are punching or punch/kick—are impressive tools in any fighter's arsenal.

In the following photos, Rich Franklin demonstrates a four-step combination that starts with a jab and finishes with a devastating kick.

(Photos courtesy Mickey Suttiratana)

Notable Fights

(Photo courtesy Zuffa, LLC)

August 17, 2006: Red Rock Casino, Las Vegas, Nevada

When it comes to elite young welterweight contenders, you couldn't do better than a matchup between Judo ace Karo Parisyan and grappling standout Diego Sanchez. So when Sanchez and Parisyan locked horns in a UFC Fight Night main event in August 2006, it was a bout that you could show to skeptics and say "this is what mixed martial arts is all about." And though the unbeaten Sanchez's true arrival as one of the best welterweights in the world came at Parisyan's expense via decision, "The Heat" should never hang his head for a performance that saw him land his patented Judo throws on Sanchez and continue to battle, even as the seemingly indefatigable Albuquerque native kept attacking for 15 torrid minutes. If you can't appreciate this fight for its technical and visceral brilliance, you need to find another sport to watch.

Defending the Takedown

As fighters unload their strikes, they may be thinking ahead to either the clinch or the takedown. Their opponent may be thinking the same thing. As such, fighters need to understand the best and easiest ways to defend against the takedown.

One of the most basic elements to defending against a takedown is to employ the sprawl. As an opponent enters to get a takedown, the fighter should look to check with his hips to disrupt the opponent's momentum and balance. The defender will also pull his legs back and away. This then leaves the fighter's body weight on top of the opponent's back. The fighter has, in effect, sprawled on top of the opponent, rendering his takedown attempt pretty much useless.

For the savvy fighter, a basic understanding of throws and how they work is essential for defending against them. In order to throw someone effectively, the person throwing has to have his center of balance, his hips, lower than the target. Done in this fashion, throws require less energy—always an important consideration in the Octagon.

To defend against a throw, then, the fighter must drop his hips and weight so that he is closer to the ground. The thrower will then have a much tougher time generating the power needed to lift and throw him.

Against a basic hip throw, for example, a wise fighter will drop his hips and shift one foot back, widening his base of support. At this point, he can apply strikes to the thrower. While hip throws tend to be rare inside the Octagon, understanding a simple technique for defending against throws in this fashion easily lends itself to the wide variety of throws and takedowns used by UFC fighters.

The Least You Need to Know

◆ Footwork enables a fighter to deliver powerful strikes, evade attacks, and position himself for victory.

◆ Timing and distancing enhance the power and effectiveness of strikes.

◆ Combinations allow a fighter to deliver a maximum number of strikes, each capitalizing on the reactions of the opponent.

◆ Basic takedown defenses include the sprawl and the hip drop to help protect against throws.

Chapter 8

Fighting from the Clinch

In This Chapter

- ◆ The Clinch
- ◆ The Striking Perspective
- ◆ The Wrestling Perspective

If no knockouts have been scored as the fighters initially engage at a distance, then both may suddenly find themselves operating in the second phase of the fight, the clinch—or sometimes they use punches to set up the clinch. This chaotic position can be characterized by incidents of calculated strikes, hard jostling for position prior to takedown attempts, resting as both fighters prepare for a fresh assault, something completely unexpected, or all of the above.

What makes the clinch so interesting is how individual fighters use it to their personal advantage. Some fighters seek to use this time to sneak close-in power shots that can really take a toll on their opponent. Other fighters try to position their hands in such a way that they can pull off a takedown. Still others will simply choose to nullify their opponent's efforts until the referee separates the fighters and starts them back across the Octagon™ from each other.

In this chapter, we take a close look at two perspectives during the clinch. First we look at how fighters who want to utilize their strikes approach the situation. Then we look at how fighters using wrestling's natural advantages seek to exploit the clinch for their own purposes.

The Striking Perspective

Now that the fighters are in the clinch and the distance between them has been chopped down, the chance for a knockout blow is reduced, although elbow strikes can certainly be used with devastating results. That said, many fighters attempt to use a series of strikes to build up enough damage to score a win in another way. They may use close-in shots, elbows, or even sneak in uppercuts or hooks to finish their opponent.

From a striker's perspective, then, the goal of the clinch is either to gain control of the neck or break the clinch and regain the distance necessary for knockout strikes.

Gaining Positional Control

Key to being able to control the fight is the quest for positional control in the clinch. As soon as both fighters clinch, it is common to see both trying to outmaneuver the other and gain the optimal position. Most UFC® fight fans are used to seeing a flurry of in-close movements happening during a clinch. But what's actually going on? As one fighter seeks to gain control, the other fighter is trying to counter that and gain control for himself. The result is a weaving pattern of arm motions that both fighters use to try to gain control or position on the inside. It is known as "pummeling."

Double Plum Clinch

One of the most common types of clinch positions is known as the "double plum." This happens when one fighter is able to position his forearms on the collarbones and neck of the other fighter. Simultaneously, he has his hands behind the head of the other fighter, clasped one over the other.

The following photo series shows a variety of angles on the double plum clinch.

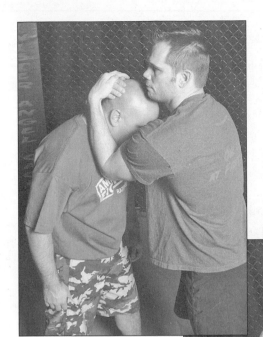

The double plum clinch.

(Photo courtesy Mickey Suttiratana)

The double plum clinch (another angle).

(Photo courtesy Mickey Suttiratana)

Close-up of the grip in the double plum clinch.

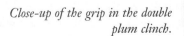

(Photo courtesy Mickey Suttiratana)

The double plum clinch is effective for a variety of reasons. The forearms pressing into the collarbones enhance control for the dominant fighter. It also has the effect of concaving the other fighter's body, resulting in less structural stability.

This is different from "hollowing," which refers to the person in control of the clinch. The hips of the "clincher" are slightly back and he is on the balls of his feet. Keeping his hips away makes it more difficult for his opponent to grab him, and staying on the balls of his feet allows for quicker movements in turning and kneeing.

Forearm position in the double plum clinch.

(Photo courtesy Mickey Suttiratana)

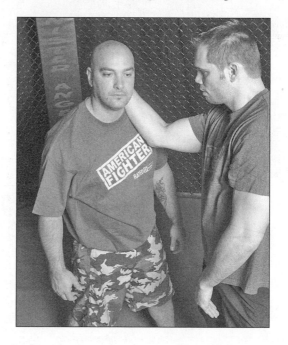

At the same time, the two hands behind the opponent's head offer the controlling fighter a fantastic means of control. The old adage "where the head goes, the body follows" truly applies here. While he controls the head, the dominant fighter has the ability to twist and turn his opponent, keeping him off-balance and open to strikes.

Using the forearm to control in the double plum clinch.

(Photo courtesy Mickey Suttiratana)

Controlling the head in the double plum clinch.

(Photo courtesy Mickey Suttiratana)

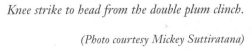

Knee strike to head from the double plum clinch.

(Photo courtesy Mickey Suttiratana)

The real goal of controlling the head with two hands, however, is to push the head down into range for knee strikes and a potential knockout. Or, to use the head to turn the body and land effective strikes to the ribs.

It's important to note that the hands must be around the neck, pulling the upper body forward and down. Keeping the elbows tight keeps the opponent trapped. The forearms act as a vice and the head should not slip through.

Attacking in the Clinch

Gaining control in the clinch, from a striking perspective, is critical to continued use of effective strikes. But even as fighters are vying for that control, opportunities exist provided the fighters are alert to their potential.

As with any opportunity, it's always a matter of who seizes upon it first. And in the chaos of a fight, seeing the chances often can be tough.

Using Punches

Certain UFC fighters, Randy Couture, for example, use a single plum clinch so they have the freedom to punch with their other hand. In this case, one hand rests on top of the opponent's head to manipulate him around, open him up for strikes, or just keep him off-balance.

At this point, it's entirely feasible for a savvy fighter to use hooks or uppercuts to level his opponent. And if the opponent gets wise to what's going on and tries to defend against the single plum, the dominating fighter simply can switch sides—that is, he can grab the other side of the opponent and punch with his other hand. The effect can be devastating.

Fighters often call this technique "dirty boxing" and it was a favored tactic of UFC great Randy Couture, who used it to great effect in many of his fights.

FIGHTER FACTS

One of the ways UFC fighters defend against the double plum clinch is by snaking their arms through the other fighter's hold. By using one of the hands to push back against the other fighter's neck or face, they can inhibit any attempts to pull their own head down. The danger in using both hands to defend against this, however, is that it leaves the rest of the torso open to attack.

Using Knees

As mentioned before, the key goal of using a double plum clinch is to force the opponent's head down into range for knee strikes. Bouncing a couple of knees off the face of an opponent can certainly alter their desire to remain in the fight.

But even if the fighter hasn't gotten the opponent's head down, he can use knee strikes on other parts of the opponent's body. Specifically, if the opponent is able to defend against the double plum clinch, the dominant fighter can use his knees to strike into the rib cage of the opponent.

Using knee strikes to the body from the double plum clinch.

(Photo courtesy Mickey Suttiratana)

More knee strikes to the body from the double plum clinch.

(Photo courtesy Mickey Suttiratana)

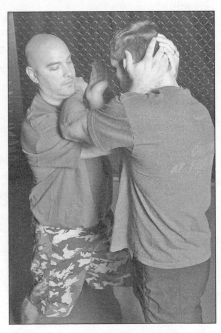

Countering the double plum clinch.

(Photo courtesy Mickey Suttiratana)

Using Elbows

More prevalent than fists, fighters often look to employ their elbows at the close-in range of clinches. From a simple standpoint, the single-joint strike of the elbow imparts more power in the confined range of the clinch. Using a fist in the same situation requires more distance to impart equal force. And often, that distance is simply not there.

At the same time, elbows when bent are one of the toughest striking surfaces on the human body. They can withstand tremendous abuse without damage. Hitting an elbow off the bony face of an opponent is far more likely to hurt the opponent than the fighter throwing the elbow.

While elbows are quite powerful, employing them in the course of a clinch can be difficult. Both fighters can feel the movements of the other and make adjustments accordingly. Elbow strikes need to be set up in order to prove effective. This can be challenging.

Elbow strikes in the clinch.

(Photo courtesy Mickey Suttiratana)

Defending the Takedown

For a fighter who primarily relies on his striking skills to win the bout, the clinch can represent a dangerous area. If he is facing a fighter who excels at wrestling or submissions, the striking savvy fighter knows his opponent will be looking to take him down to the mat and go to work on him there. Defending against the takedown then becomes of paramount importance.

It's important to note that in order to "shoot" properly, the fighter looking to do so must be at the right range. Trying to shoot covering too much distance is suicide. A wise fighter will simply knee him in the face as he shoots. Most fighters looking to shoot keep themselves at arm's length, knowing from that distance their chances of success are much higher.

Defender hand position start as opponent shoots.

(Photo courtesy Mickey Suttiratana)

Defender hand position finish as opponent shoots.

(Photo courtesy Mickey Suttiratana)

Defender stuffs opponent's momentum with his arm and hip.

(Photo courtesy Mickey Suttiratana)

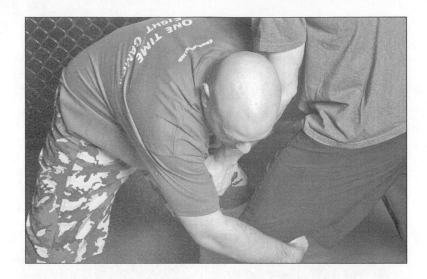

If the fighter gets in on the defending fighter's hips, the standing fighter's second line of defense is the sprawl. The key to an effective sprawl is for the defending fighter to keep his hips (his center of gravity) away from the attacker's arms. Using his own weight and hands, he can then drive his opponent into the canvas.

The Sprawl.

(Photo courtesy Mickey Suttiratana)

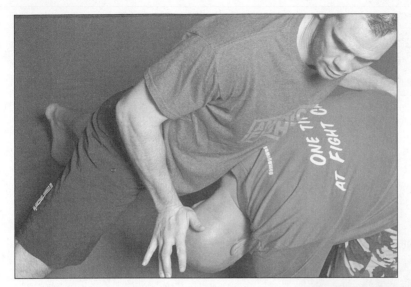

Pressing down on the head in the sprawl.

(Photo courtesy Mickey Suttiratana)

This is one reason a lot of fighters look to use the cage to their advantage during takedown attempts. By backing their opponent up against the Octagon and then attempting to take him down, the defending fighter is unable to back out with his legs and sprawl. From a strategic standpoint, fighters will look to use the Octagon to maximize their takedown attempts. The Octagon also keeps fighters from falling out, unlike a boxing ring.

Using the cage to help the takedown.

(Photo courtesy Mickey Suttiratana)

| PRO-FILES | *Heavyweight Contender: Mirko Cro Cop* |

(Photo courtesy Zuffa, LLC)

Fighting out of: Vinkovci, Croatia
Born: 9/10/74
Height: 6'2"
Weight: 220 lbs.
Weightclass: Heavyweight
Top UFC heavyweight contender

Perhaps the most feared striker in all of mixed martial arts, Mirko Cro Cop is known for a left kick to the head that is nothing short of devastating. His other standup attacks are nothing to take lightly either, and after a successful run in Japan, this former Anti-Terrorist squad officer and current member of the Croatian Parliament has come to the United States to take on the UFC's best. In his first UFC bout at UFC 67 in February of 2007, Cro Cop stopped previously unbeaten Eddie Sanchez in the first round.

Breaking the Clinch to Strike

A lot of fighters who prefer striking will seek to get out of a clinch as soon as possible. By gaining distance again, they are able to resort to their bread-and-butter strikes to win the match. But while they may be desperate to break out of the clinch, they also know that doing so without covering their escape may lead to their own downfall.

The Wrestling Perspective

On the other side of the equation, fighters who enjoy wrestling or submissions will try to use the clinch to their advantage. Their goal then is to get double underhooks on their opponent, which will enable them to get a takedown. In this case they will use pummeling to accomplish this from a clinch.

In order to achieve this goal, fighters preferring wrestling techniques must be wary as they work through the pummel to get the advantage.

Double underhooks.

(Photo courtesy Mickey Suttiratana)

Gaining Positional Control

As with striking from the clinch, effectively wrestling from the clinch also means that the fighter must work hard to gain the optimal position over his opponent. For a wrestler or submissions specialist, this point of absolute control starts in one position and works into another.

Over-Under Clinch

This position simply refers to where a fighter's arms are in relation to his opponent. Each fighter has one arm "over" one of his opponent's arms. In other words, all other factors being equal, the fighters are at something of a standstill in terms of position.

The over-under clinch.

(Photo courtesy Mickey Suttiratana)

From this over-under, fighters will try to work using the pummel drill to better their position and move into the next step of clinching from the wrestling perspective. The process of gaining the advantage and progressing can take, relatively speaking, quite a while—especially since so many fighters understand how to pummel now.

Double Underhooks

If the wrestling specialist is able to gain advantage and move from the pummel into the next phase of the clinch, he now is looking for "double underhooks." This is another wrestling term used to describe the action of getting both hands under the arms of your opponent and grasping them behind his back. It appears that one fighter is giving a front bear hug to the other, but in reality, this is a highly dominant position that allows the fighter who has achieved double underhooks to throw or take his opponent down to the ground.

Start position for double underhooks.

(Photo courtesy Mickey Suttiratana)

End position for double underhooks.

(Photo courtesy Mickey Suttiratana)

The opponent who finds himself caught in this position may attempt a number of counters, including double "overhooks." Other fighters may try striking or going for their opponent's head to try and stop the inevitable takedown.

Double overhooks 1.

(Photo courtesy Mickey Suttiratana)

PRO-FILES   *Diego "Nightmare" Sanchez*

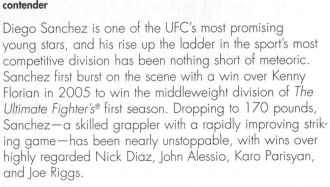

(Photo courtesy Zuffa, LLC)

Fighting out of: Albuquerque, New Mexico
Born: 12/31/81
Height: 5'11"
Weight: 170 lbs.
Weightclass: Welterweight
Winner of season one of *The Ultimate Fighter®*; current welterweight contender

Diego Sanchez is one of the UFC's most promising young stars, and his rise up the ladder in the sport's most competitive division has been nothing short of meteoric. Sanchez first burst on the scene with a win over Kenny Florian in 2005 to win the middleweight division of *The Ultimate Fighter's®* first season. Dropping to 170 pounds, Sanchez—a skilled grappler with a rapidly improving striking game—has been nearly unstoppable, with wins over highly regarded Nick Diaz, John Alessio, Karo Parisyan, and Joe Riggs.

Notable Fights

Matt Hughes and Georges St-Pierre at UFC 65.

(Photo courtesy Zuffa, LLC)

November 18, 2006: ARCO Arena, Sacramento, California

The highly anticipated rematch between Matt Hughes and Georges St-Pierre made this bout one of the most exciting for the entire year of 2006. Despite having beaten St-Pierre nearly

two years earlier, no one seemed ready to call this fight a sure thing for Hughes.

Indeed, St-Pierre had reinvented himself during the time away from Hughes. The Canadian came out looking focused and intent and proceeded to hunt Hughes throughout the first round. St-Pierre scored two inadvertent low kicks during the opening frame. Hughes would later admit one of them had caused his leg to go numb.

After being warned by referee "Big John" McCarthy, St-Pierre landed a demolishing punch on Hughes and followed with a vicious left hook that took Hughes to the mat shortly before the end of the round.

In round two, St-Pierre again stalked Hughes, stuffing his takedown attempts and setting him up with an inside leg kick fake that covered a stunning high kick to the head, flooring Hughes. St-Pierre then rained punches and elbows down on Hughes.

At 1:25 of round two, referee McCarthy called a halt to the fight and St-Pierre won by technical knockout to become the UFC Welterweight Champion.

Going for the Takedown

What a UFC fighter who prefers wrestling or submitting his opponents wants most is to take the fight to the ground. A fighter can go for a takedown by shooting or from the clinch.

From the clinch, then, there are a number of takedown possibilities for the ground-fighter to work with. Let's take a look at several of them.

Single Leg Takedown

The first option for UFC fighters is the single leg takedown. (Please note: the single leg takedown can also be done from a shot.) In this technique, the fighter grabs one of the legs of his opponent, normally using both of his hands, and then takes him down to the ground.

There are a variety of ways to upset the balance of the opponent in order to take him down using the single leg takedown. But normally, one part of the leg is pulled in one direction while the fighter uses his shoulder or upper body to force the upper part of the opponent's leg, and therefore the rest of his body, toward the ground. Other methods include grabbing the ankle and manipulating at that joint or pressing the leg high up toward the groin as a means of upsetting the balance.

The following pictures illustrate the single leg takedown.

The single leg takedown.

(Photo courtesy Mickey Suttiratana)

The danger in using a single leg takedown is that it unduly exposes the fighter's head to counter strikes. The single leg takedown may also be defended against by using the sprawl.

Double Leg Takedown

Similar to the single leg takedown, the "double," as it's sometimes referred to, involves one fighter wrapping both of his arms around both of the opponent's legs. He then drives his opponent to the ground in a number of ways.

The double leg takedown.

(Photo courtesy Mickey Suttiratana)

He may opt to lift his opponent up and then slam him back down to the ground, often on the opponent's back. He may also yank back on the opponent's legs while using his shoulder and upper torso to drive the opponent back onto his seat.

As with the single, a fighter may use the sprawl to defend against the double leg takedown as soon as his opponent shoots in from the clinch and tries it. The fighter may then elect to use strikes to punish his opponent once the sprawl has proven an effective defense.

As we'll see in a later chapter, the guillotine choke is also an effective defense against the double leg takedown.

Wrestling Throw

Many UFC fighters prefer using wrestling-based throws for the simple reason that wrestling throws are easier to pull off in the Octagon. Since the rules specifically forbid uniforms, the benefits gained by being able to use the uniform against the opponent during a Judo-type throw are nullified. While there are certainly skilled fighters who do not need to rely on the Judo uniform in order to execute Judo-type throws, most will opt to use whatever is easier to apply in the chaotic flow of an Octagon fight. Judo Gene LeBell, and the fighters he trains, are fantastic examples of fighters who can throw regardless of attire.

Starting the wrestling throw.

(Photo courtesy Mickey Suttiratana)

Middle position for the throw.

(Photo courtesy Mickey Suttiratana)

Finishing the throw.

(Photo courtesy Mickey Suttiratana)

For today's UFC fighters, the clinch is the bridge between the standup game and the world of takedowns and groundfighting. Only by mastering the give-and-take flow of jockeying for position in the clinch can fighters hope to effectively set their opponents up for the next assault.

The Least You Need to Know

- The clinch enables fighters to work their specialties in order to get the takedown or knockout.

- Gaining positional advantage is the key to winning while in the clinch.

- Fighters may elect to strike from within the clinch or break it to gain distance for their strikes.

- Groundfighters look to gain a position where they can clinch their hands behind their opponents back to look for a throw.

- The clinch is the bridge between standup fighting and groundfighting.

Shooting for the Takedown

In This Chapter

- ◆ Setting Up the Takedown
- ◆ Level Changing
- ◆ Staying Protected
- ◆ Single Leg Takedown
- ◆ Double Leg Takedown

Once a fighter spots an opportunity in the midst of the fight and decides he's going for the takedown, there are several factors to consider. A fighter needs to be especially aware of how he intends to enter for that takedown. He also needs to consider how his opponent may try to defend against his action, or even counter his attempts.

Shooting for the takedown then is a risky gambit for any fighter. It's not enough to simply shoot and hope for the best. There's science at work there that helps give savvy fighters an edge over less experienced opponents.

In this chapter, we take a look at how a wise fighter sets up his opponent for the take-down and then goes about getting it once it's in sight. We examine ways fighters keep themselves covered as they shoot, how they upset their opponent's balance and more. Shooting, in this case, isn't done with the blast of a shotgun, but with the precision of a sniper's rifle.

Setting Up the Takedown

Any attempt at a takedown needs to be preceded by another technique or movement so the opponent has as little chance as possible at detecting the takedown attempt. Otherwise, the opponent will be able to defend himself against the takedown, or possibly even counter it. You should also note that oftentimes the first takedown attempt is not always successful. When you see someone like Matt Hughes drive his opponent against the fence, he may be working on his second, third, or even fourth takedown in a series. Sometimes setups for takedowns are other takedowns or feints of takedowns.

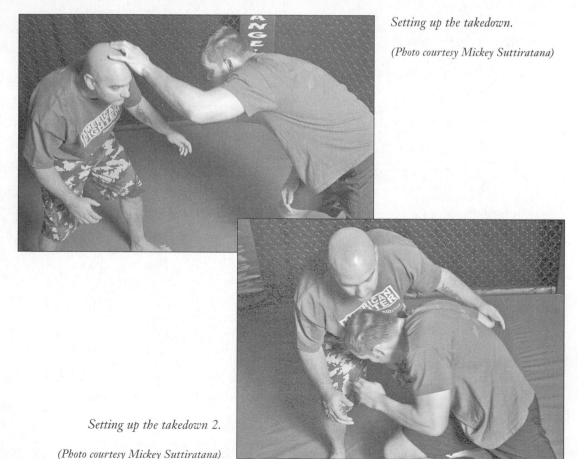

Setting up the takedown.

(Photo courtesy Mickey Suttiratana)

Setting up the takedown 2.

(Photo courtesy Mickey Suttiratana)

Shooting for a takedown can be risky. As we've seen, there are a number of ways savvy fighters protect themselves, and there are a number of easy defenses opponents can employ to thwart the takedown attempt. For this reason, when a fighter decides to shoot, he must make sure he has the best chance possible of pulling it off.

Using Strikes

Many fighters will use a strike or series of strikes to cover their takedown attempts. By launching a couple of close-in hooks or elbows, fighters can get the opponents reacting to the strikes. As their bodies pitch one way or another, their rhythm and balance are upset. This then enables a fighter to shoot and get the takedown, preferably before their opponent realizes what's happening.

Depending on which stance the opponent is in, the ability to shoot and get the takedown may vary. Wrestling stances, for example, are much lower. Remember: the key to getting a takedown is getting your center of gravity lower than your opponent's.

In the following photos, notice how Rich uses strikes up top in the clinch, and then level changes as his opponent reacts and shoots for the takedown.

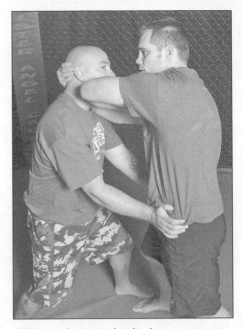

Elbow strike up in the clinch.

(Photo courtesy Mickey Suttiratana)

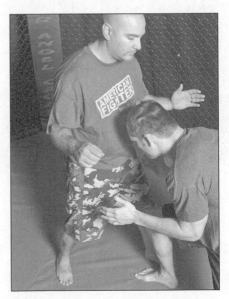

Level changing to get the takedown.

(Photo courtesy Mickey Suttiratana)

Using the Pummel

Another way fighters can cover their takedown attempt is to work off the pummel. As they go through the motions of vying for control, good fighters will interrupt the rhythm here and then shoot low, or clinch and look for a throw. Sometimes again, they will throw an elbow or hook into the mix just as they start to shoot, for added protection.

Notice how Rich works off the pummel drill in the following photographs. As he and his opponent work to gain control, he upsets the rhythm by suddenly shooting low.

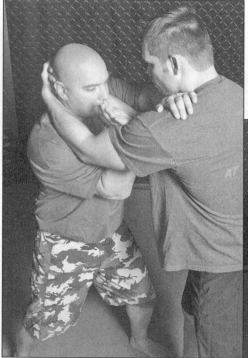

Working the pummel.

(Photo courtesy Mickey Suttiratana)

Shooting low for the takedown.

(Photo courtesy Mickey Suttiratana)

Using Bodyweight

One of the more interesting ways to set up a takedown is to use a varying degree of bodyweight during the clinch. In this technique, as the fighters grapple about in the clinch, the fighter about to try the takedown will step back and drop his weight. His opponent's response may be to pull back and up to resist the move. As he pulls back and up, the fighter setting up the takedown can then "ride" that energy back in and shoot effectively.

This is also seen to some effect when fighters pummel. As previously discussed, fighters will be moving their arms trying to get positional control on the inside. Simultaneously, however, they are also shifting their weight and their opponent's. They are, in effect, fighting for position with their legs as much as their arms.

Leaning on the opponent.

(Photo courtesy Mickey Suttiratana)

Going for the takedown.

(Photo courtesy Mickey Suttiratana)

The fighter setting up his opponent may also crowd the other fighter using his body. As he moves in, trying to overwhelm the opponent, the opponent may back up, trying to get distance and regain some control. At this point, the fighter can use the opponent's reaction to cover his takedown attempt.

Level Changing

Once the fighter is in the midst of shooting for the takedown, there is one vital point he must be sure he understands in order to successfully get his opponent down. A wise fighter knows he must "change his level"—meaning very simply that he must get his center of gravity lower than his opponent's center of gravity.

Simple physics demands that in order to move a heavy object, you must have the bulk of your mass lower than the object you are trying to move. The same is true for a fighter looking for a takedown. His opponent's mass is on one level. The fighter attempting the takedown must make sure his mass is lower than his opponent's in order to move him, or in this case, take him down.

Changing levels in a mixed martial arts competition is different from the same tactic seen in wrestling matches. In wrestling, both competitors are already hunkered down observing the other. Many times, a wrestler will have to virtually get himself on the ground in order to get lower than his opponent.

But in a UFC® match, both fighters are standing "taller." This means that a fighter in a mixed martial arts match needs only get lower than his opponent by a smaller margin. In many cases, this can mean the fighter simply needs to bend his knees and sink down a fraction, and then he will be able to topple his opponent.

In the following pictures, Rich demonstrates how this idea works when using the cage against an opponent. In the first picture, Rich stacks his opponent. In the next frame, he changes his level, getting his hips lower than his opponents. And then Rich gets the takedown.

Stacking the opponent.

(Photo courtesy Mickey Suttiratana)

Changing the level.

(Photo courtesy Mickey Suttiratana)

Rich gets the takedown.

(Photo courtesy Mickey Suttiratana)

The same idea of level changing applies regardless of how a fighter is attempting the takedown. In order to pull off a wrestling takedown, a Judo-style throw, or any other means of bringing an opponent down, the fighter must ensure he is lower than his opponent.

 FIGHTER FACTS

Notice how fighters understand that their center of gravity is fixed in their hips. When the level changes, they know that the key is to drop their hips while keeping their backs fairly straight. Bending over is a serious mistake and compromises the fighter's balance and ability to get a takedown. It also opens them up to serious attacks from their opponent.

Staying Protected

Assuming the fighter has set up the takedown effectively and has changed his level, he is now in the midst of shooting. But the takedown is still not guaranteed to be successful if the fighter simply speeds in unaware. It's crucial for the fighter to be able to protect himself even as he shoots.

The best way to keep covered is for a fighter to keep his arms inside as he shoots. In other words, he simply doesn't shoot with his arms extended as if he's going in for a big hug around his opponent's legs. Instead, the fighter keeps his guard up until the very last second, opening his arms just enough to secure them around either one or both of the opponent's legs.

Keeping the hands on the inside.

(Photo courtesy Mickey Suttiratana)

PRO-FILES | **Rising Star: Kenny "KenFlo" Florian**

(Photo courtesy Zuffa, LLC)

Fighting out of: Boston, Massachusetts
Born: 5/26/76
Height: 5'10"
Weight: 155 lbs.
Weightclass: Lightweight
The Ultimate Fighter® season one finalist; former UFC lightweight title challenger

A native of Westwood, Massachusetts, Kenny Florian has impressed UFC fans with his incredible endurance and excellent chin. A gifted grappler who enjoys looking for the submission or choke hold, Kenny is just as comfortable with his striking game, which is based around his Muay Thai background. His notable fights in the past have included several wins by submission and a gutsy five-round loss via unanimous decision to Sean Sherk at *UFC 64: Unstoppable* that won him legions of new fans for his ability to go the distance with Sherk while never yielding in his desire to win the fight.

Shooting in this way helps ensure very little chance of an opponent being able to catch the fighter unaware with a counter. But there have been plenty of examples of UFC fighters who chose to shoot in with their arms extended. Inevitably, a wise opponent has simply lifted his knee and caught them as they shot in. Such a counter can be devastating and end the fight in a second.

Single Leg Takedown

As we saw in the last chapter, one of the quickest takedowns is the single leg. In this technique, a fighter wraps his hands around one of the opponent's legs and then forces him to the ground either by driving him back and down, or by lifting up and then toppling him.

The single leg takedown.

(Photo courtesy Mickey Suttiratana)

If nothing else is available, a single can be an effective means of getting an opponent down on the ground. Most fighters would probably opt to use a double leg takedown, since it offers more control and better protection for them.

Double Leg Takedown

Most fighters aim to wrap the legs around the knees, possibly locking them out as they wrap them up. Locked out knees cannot help maintain the balance of the opponent, and it's easier to then bring them down to the ground. In the following pictures, Rich changes his level to drop low and secure his hands around both of his opponent's legs. He then lifts up and gets the takedown, toppling his opponent.

Shooting for the takedown is the last step of the second part of the fight. We're leaving the standup fight behind now and heading down to the ground. It's a place where anything can happen. Where fights are won and lost. And where savvy fighters know they have to be at the top of their game if they hope to emerge victorious.

The double leg takedown.

(Photo courtesy Mickey Suttiratana)

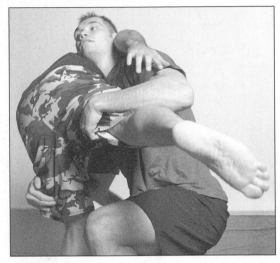

The finish.

(Photo courtesy Mickey Suttiratana)

PRO-FILES Quinton "Rampage" Jackson

(Photo courtesy Zuffa, LLC)

Fighting out of: Memphis, Tennessee
Born: 6/20/78
Height: 6'1"
Weight: 205 lbs.
Weightclass: Light Heavyweight
UFC Light Heavyweight Champion

One of the most charismatic figures ever to step into the Octagon™, Memphis-born Quinton "Rampage" Jackson arrived in the UFC in 2007 after a successful stint fighting in Japan, and immediately made his mark with a knockout win over the first man to beat him, Marvin Eastman, at UFC 67. An aggressive fighter known for his wrestling, a willingness to go to war standing, and his trademark bodyslams, Jackson stunned the world in May of 2007 when he knocked out Chuck Liddell in the first round at UFC 71 to win the UFC Light Heavyweight Championship.

Notable Fights

Kendall Grove vs. Ed Herman at The Ultimate Fighter® 3 Finale.

(Photo courtesy Zuffa, LLC)

June 24, 2006: Las Vegas, Nevada

The live finale of the third season of *The Ultimate Fighter®* brought a new level of excitement as fans tuned in to watch an amazing fight between Ed Herman and Kendall Grove unfold on Spike TV.

In the first round, both fighters came out swinging but quickly went to the ground, each looking to impose their own grappling holds on the other. By all accounts, Herman won the first round after getting Grove into numerous holds.

Grove turned the tables in the second round, by again going to the ground and using the cage to his advantage. He was the one putting Herman into the holds and locks this round, although with the skill levels of both fighters extremely high, no hold seemed to last long as they both showed their incredible escape talents as well.

In the third and final round, both fighters—now visibly tired from the struggle—managed to hang on through an incredible seesaw flurry of action that again saw both fighters working holds on the other only to have them reversed and reversed again.

At the end of the match, a narrow decision gave the match to Grove, who won a six-figure UFC contract. But UFC president Dana White then awarded Herman a six-figure deal as well, saying that both fighters had proven themselves extremely worthy of joining the UFC roster.

The Least You Need to Know

◆ Strikes, bodyweight, and rhythm interruption are key methods for setting up the takedown.

◆ To get a takedown, a fighter must ensure his center of gravity is lower than his opponent's.

◆ When shooting, a fighter's hands should always be kept on the inside or else he is vulnerable to counter attacks.

◆ Single and double leg takedowns are among the most common means of getting an opponent to the ground.

Part 4

When the Fight Goes to the Ground

At last the fighters have gone to the ground. It's here that they must be especially aware of how quickly the fight can be lost. In this part, we examine what happens on the ground from two perspectives: the fighter on top and the fighter on the bottom. Each position has strengths and limitations. We'll look at them all.

Chapter 10

The Guard

In This Chapter

- The Guard
- The Top Position Perspective
- The Bottom Position Perspective

We're at the third stage of the fight: the battle on the ground. We've progressed from the standup to the clinch to the takedown and now at last, the fighters find themselves positioning for victory on the ground. Please remember that there are a number of different ways the fighters will end up on the ground. For the purposes of this book, we've sketched the flow of an imaginary fight. But as any good fighter understands, things in the Octagon™ are never carved in stone.

In this chapter, we'll look at the Guard, the defensive position utilized by the fighter who ends up being taken down. We'll also examine how each position appears from the top and bottom perspective, exploring what each fighter might be looking to achieve in their quest for victory.

First Things First …

Oftentimes when a fighter is taken down, they will look to "establish guard" on the ground. The reason for this is simple: the guard is the most "equal" of ground positions.

Some fighters, particularly jiu-jitsu fighters who are supremely confident in their groundfighting ability, or fighters unable to secure a takedown in another fashion, may opt to "jump guard," that is, drag or pull the opponent to the canvas on top of him. While this isn't seen very often nowadays, like everything else, the possibility always exists that a fighter will try it if the opportunity presents itself.

As the opponent being thrown is looking to establish the guard, the fighter doing the takedown will look to "clear the legs" in order to establish a cross mount or at least a half guard. Again, there are innumerable positions a fighter may end up in as they go to the ground. For the purposes of this book, however, we'll assume both fighters end up in the guard.

As with everything, there are advantages and disadvantages to being on the top and bottom in the guard. Today's UFC® fighters take great steps to fully understand the benefits and drawbacks of each position, knowing full well that the more they train to work from both perspectives, the better prepared they'll be in the Octagon.

Being on Top, in the Guard

The fighter caught in the guard does not want to be there, but will commonly have to settle for this position after securing the takedown. The top man has to stay parallel to the bottom man. The elbows must be in and he must keep the legs that are wrapped around him from moving up his body. If not, he is vulnerable to a submission attempt. In addition, he has to maintain a solid base so he is not swept or rolled into mount position.

The top man has three options in order of difficulty. The first is to strike, which is the easiest in terms of technique. He will posture up to create space and then reign down blows with the fists and elbows. The second is to pass the guard and move into a better position, which allows him to continue to strike but also opens up a vast number of submission options. The third is to attempt a submission from within the guard itself, but this is very unlikely against a UFC caliber fighter … because his submission options are limited, and require him to give up position.

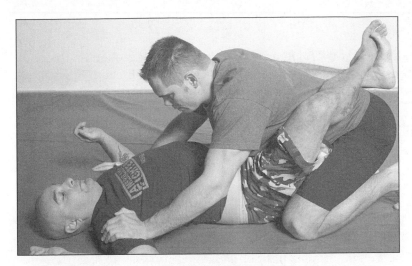

In the guard.

(Photo courtesy Mickey Suttiratana)

FIGHTER FACTS

The top position fighter may opt to sit back and attempt an ankle lock if the bottom man does not have his legs locked or is utilizing the open guard. It's possible. But not likely. The reason is simple: once a fighter earns that top position, he wants to keep it. Sitting back for the ankle lock compromises his position, opens him to counters, and also may enable his opponent to gain the top position.

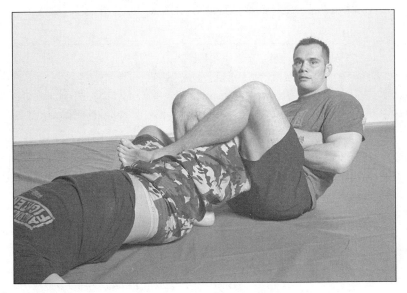

The ankle lock.

(Photo courtesy Mickey Suttiratana)

Ground-and-Pound

Many top position fighters can look to immediately establish their ground-and-pound game, which can soften up, cut, and even KO the bottom man. Fighters on top will look to apply a series of body shots and then possibly come over the top with an elbow to the face or head. They'll work a rhythm of strikes: body-body-head, body-body-elbow, and so on. This is the easiest offense to use in terms of technique.

Starting the ground-and-pound from the guard.

(Photo courtesy Mickey Suttiratana)

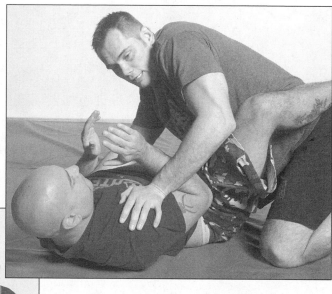

Punching from a standing guard.

(Photo courtesy Mickey Suttiratana)

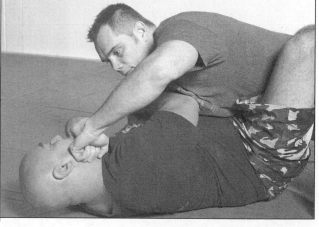

Landing the punch from the guard.

(Photo courtesy Mickey Suttiratana)

If the fighter chooses to use the ground-and-pound strategy, he must be sure that he is doing damage to his opponent. If it appears to the referee that no damage is being done, the referee will most likely stand the fight back up. Considering all that they've done to get their opponent to the ground, most fighters will do their best to inflict some damage and avoid being stood up. Elbow strikes are the best way to achieve big damage when using the ground-and-pound strategy. Fighters may also look to improve their position if it seems they are not achieving any damage.

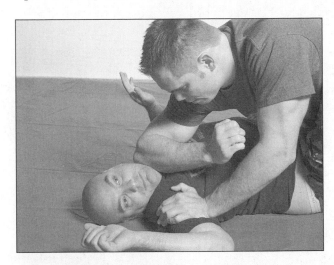

Landing the elbow strike from the guard.

(Photo courtesy Mickey Suttiratana)

PRO-FILES   *Rising Star: Forrest Griffin*

(Photo courtesy Zuffa, LLC)

Fighting out of: Athens, Georgia
Born: 3/16/79
Height: 6'3"
Weight: 205 lbs.
Weightclass: Light Heavyweight
Winner of season one of *The Ultimate Fighter®*

A former Georgia police officer loved by fight fans not only for his aggressive fighting style but for his humble demeanor and quirky sense of humor, Forrest Griffin may have done more for the emergence of the UFC in recent years than any other fighter due to his performance against Stephan Bonnar in *The Ultimate Fighter®* season one finale in April 2005, a bout that was the first event televised live on cable in MMA history. Since that epic battle, Griffin has continued to delight fans with every bout, win or lose, with his only defeats coming at the hands of fellow top contenders Tito Ortiz and Keith Jardine.

Improve Position

The third option for top position fighters is to look for a chance to improve their position. The guard is, at best, a 50-50 proposition with both fighters being somewhat equal in terms of choices. An experienced fighter will look to position himself where he has more control.

To do so, he will pass the guard and move up the body, into the half guard position (we cover the half guard in Chapter 11). But in order to move into the half guard, the fighter also will have to cover his advance. In this case, strikes play an integral part of any movement. Again, a lot of fighters will look to apply a series of strikes and move in the spaces between the strikes.

Depending on how the fighters are positioned, there are several ways to pass the guard. Beginning from the standing position, the following photo series illustrates various ways to accomplish this.

Passing the guard from standing position 1.

(Photo courtesy Mickey Suttiratana)

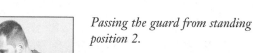

Passing the guard from standing position 2.

(Photo courtesy Mickey Suttiratana)

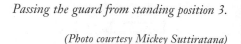

Passing the guard from standing position 3.

(Photo courtesy Mickey Suttiratana)

Standing alternative 1.

(Photo courtesy Mickey Suttiratana)

And here is how a fighter passes the guard while on the ground.

Passing the guard from the ground 1.

(Photo courtesy Mickey Suttiratana)

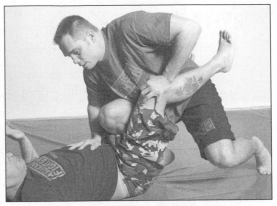

Passing the guard from the ground 2.

(Photo courtesy Mickey Suttiratana)

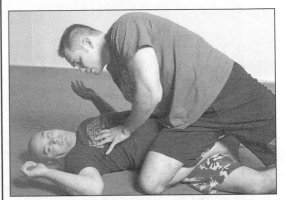

Passing the guard from the ground 3.

(Photo courtesy Mickey Suttiratana)

Passing the guard ending position.

(Photo courtesy Mickey Suttiratana)

Another way fighters may look to improve their position is to "stack" their opponent up against the Octagon cage. As we've seen previously, using the cage in this fashion can be beneficial in that it limits the mobility of the opponent.

When the fighters are on the ground, using the cage also can limit mobility as well as the ability of an opponent to ward off the ground-and-pound, submission, or positional improvement strategies.

PRO-FILES **Tito Ortiz**

(Photo courtesy Zuffa, LLC)

Fighting out of: Huntington Beach, California
Born: 1/23/75
Height: 6'2"
Weight: 205 lbs.
Weightclass: Light Heavyweight
Former UFC Light Heavyweight Champion; coach on season three of
The Ultimate Fighter®

Despite his punishing ground-and-pound style and his nickname as 'The Huntington Beach Bad Boy," Tito Ortiz garnered a legion of fans for himself for another reason after his stint as a coach on season three of *The Ultimate Fighter®* reality series in 2006. After taking the time to groom a new crop of MMA stars, Ortiz got back to his own business inside the Octagon, and he defeated Forrest Griffin and Ken Shamrock (twice) before falling short in a gallant effort against Light Heavyweight Champ Chuck Liddell at UFC 66 in December of 2006. In 2007, Ortiz will again try to climb the mountain to regain his belt.

Submissions

Another option the top position fighter has is to go for some type of submission. From the guard, his submission choices are severely limited. As we've seen, he can attempt an ankle lock, but that involves giving up his dominant top position. The following pictures illustrate three different angles of the ankle lock.

On the Bottom

Like the top position fighter, the fighter on the bottom also has a number of goals he will try to achieve from his perspective. Most likely the bottom position fighter will want to either tie up the top fighter so the fight gets stood back up, obtain some sort of submission on the top position fighter, or reverse his position so that he is on top.

The possibility also exists of throwing strikes at the fighter caught in his guard, but position limits power and getting into a striking match with the top man will begin a losing situation. Elbows can be effective, as well as throwing strikes in conjunction with a submission such as a triangle choke.

Tying Things Up

As the top position fighter attempts to control the arms of the bottom fighter— specifically the biceps—the bottom fighter often will respond by knocking the top fighter's arms off of him. Usually this is done by lifting up or striking up under the top fighter's arms. The appearance is very much like doing the pummel drill on the ground, as we saw in the previous section with regard to the top position fighter attempting to gain control.

If the bottom position fighter knows he will be on the receiving end of a ground-and-pound strategy, he may opt to tie up the top fighter. Once the referee sees that nothing is happening, he will intervene and stand both fighters back up.

One of the easiest ways to tie up the fight is by reducing or eliminating the amount of space between the fighters. Because the top position fighter needs room to be able to generate momentum and launch strikes, the fighter on the bottom will work to reach up behind the top fighter's neck or head and pull his head down into the bottom fighter's chest while simultaneously trapping the punching arm.

The following photographs show how the fighter on the bottom works to tie up the fighter on top and control the space in the hopes that the fight is stood back up.

Starting to tie things up.

(Photo courtesy Mickey Suttiratana)

Mid-position for the tie-up.

(Photo courtesy Mickey Suttiratana)

End position for the tie-up.

(Photo courtesy Mickey Suttiratana)

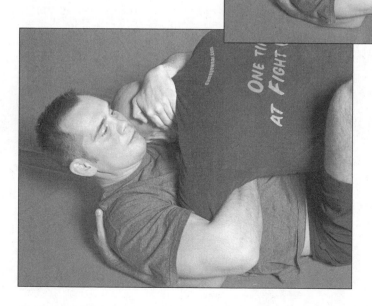

Close-up.

(Photo courtesy Mickey Suttiratana)

The top position fighter will try to create space while the bottom fighter will try to keep his body as close to his opponent's as possible. In effect, he'll wrap himself around the top fighter, limiting any type of technique. Inevitably, the referee will then step in.

Submitting

If the bottom position fighter enjoys working on the ground, he may look to acquire a submission. If he chooses to do this, the most important thing he must do is keep his hips moving at all times. Just as the top position fighter needs space to inflict his strikes, the bottom position fighter needs space in order to look for possible submissions—including armbars and triangle chokes.

Remember, there are primarily two types of guards … one in which you have your legs wrapped around your opponent, and the butterfly guard. If you decide to transition into butterfly guard, you will be looking for a reversal or standing up, not a submission. One way to accomplish this is by transitioning into another type of guard: the open guard or the butterfly guard. With the open guard, the bottom position fighter's feet are in the top fighter's hips or under his thighs. This is extremely useful in case the top position fighter rears back to throw a huge punch. The bottom position fighter can kick into his hips and move him back or at least disrupt the momentum. Once the top position fighter moves back, the bottom position fighter then has the option to stand back up.

Working to open the guard.

(Photo courtesy Mickey Suttiratana)

In the following photos, the fighter uses the open guard to escape and stand back up.

Using the open guard to escape 1.

(Photo courtesy Mickey Suttiratana)

Escaping step 2.

(Photo courtesy Mickey Suttiratana)

Escaping step 3.

(Photo courtesy Mickey Suttiratana)

Back to standing.

(Photo courtesy Mickey Suttiratana)

At this point, if the situation is favorable, the fighter can also opt to move into a choke hold.

The butterfly guard happens when the bottom position fighter has his feet under the top position fighter's thighs or in his hips. This gives the bottom position fighter leverage against the top fighter's balance. Generally speaking, a fighter in closed guard will be looking for a submission while a fighter operating in the butterfly guard will be looking to reverse his position or will be trying to stand up.

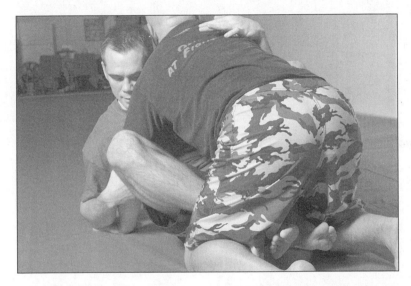

The butterfly guard.

(Photo courtesy Mickey Suttiratana)

Using either the open or the butterfly guard, the fighter on the bottom can ward off punches, and create and control space as seen in the photographs below.

Using the butterfly guard to thwart punches & create space 1.

(Photo courtesy Mickey Suttiratana)

Using the butterfly guard to thwart punches and create space 2.

(Photo courtesy Mickey Suttiratana)

Submissions from the Bottom

There are several submission choices for the bottom position fighter who is not in the butterfly guard. First and perhaps most obvious is the armbar. With both fighters vying for positional advantage, working through the pummel, and trying to control each other, the arms are a natural target. The bottom position fighter can wait and as he works through the transition, take a shot at getting the armbar. Notice here how Rich works from the guard position into an armbar.

Opening the guard as the fighter acquires the arm.

(Photo courtesy Mickey Suttiratana)

Moving into position.

(Photo courtesy Mickey Suttiratana)

Clamping down.

(Photo courtesy Mickey Suttiratana)

The triangle is another submission option that bottom fighters routinely look to acquire. Obviously, a bottom position fighter needs to be nimble enough to bring his legs into the equation, using them for the necessary leverage as he pulls the opponent's arm down and uses his legs and his opponent's own shoulder to get the choke.

Now let's take a look at the triangle in action.

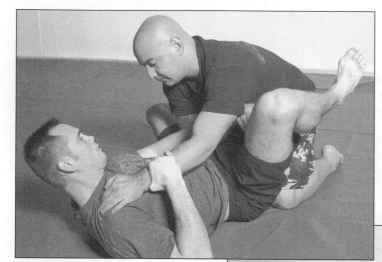

The triangle step 1.

(Photo courtesy Mickey Suttiratana)

Step 2.

(Photo courtesy Mickey Suttiratana)

And from a different angle …

Step 3.

(Photo courtesy Mickey Suttiratana)

Another submission option is the kimura, which the bottom position fighter will attempt to get by wrapping one of his arms around the head of the top fighter, pulling him close, and then going to work on his other arm until he has the lock.

By sitting up, a bottom fighter may be able to acquire the guillotine choke. After getting himself upright, he would then lean back and move his hips out to the side in order to fully execute the choke.

Here's a look at the guillotine choke.

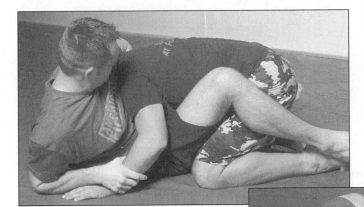

The guillotine step 1.

(Photo courtesy Mickey Suttiratana)

The guillotine step 2.

(Photo courtesy Mickey Suttiratana)

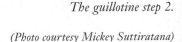

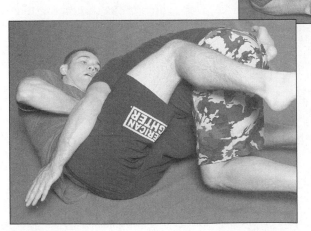

The guillotine step 3.

(Photo courtesy Mickey Suttiratana)

And from a different angle ...

Step 1.

(Photo courtesy Mickey Suttiratana)

Step 2.

(Photo courtesy Mickey Suttiratana)

Fighters on the bottom also may elect to go for a keylock, which looks something like a chicken wing type of lock. This series of photos shows how the fighter on the bottom will go about getting this lock.

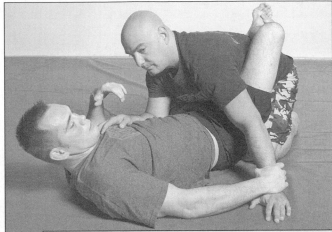

The keylock step 1.

(Photo courtesy Mickey Suttiratana)

The keylock step 2.

(Photo courtesy Mickey Suttiratana)

The keylock step 3.

(Photo courtesy Mickey Suttiratana)

Notable Fights

November 11, 2006: Hard Rock Hotel and Casino, Las Vegas, Nevada

You would think that when friends square off in combat that they would take a little something off their punches and be a little gun-shy about going for the finish. Don't tell that to middleweight up-and-comers and *The Ultimate Fighter® 4* cast members Scott Smith and Pete "Drago" Sell, who were swinging for the fences from the opening bell and who punctuated their furious exchanges with smiles and high fives.

In the second round, the torrid pace continued, but Smith appeared to be pulling ahead when Sell landed an equalizer in the form of a vicious body shot. But as Smith staggered backwards in pain, Sell rushed in recklessly and got caught with a shot on the jaw by "Hands of Steel" that ended his night. It was a Hollywood ending to an exciting war and will live on in highlight reels forever.

Reversal or Sweep

The last option the bottom position fighter has is to attempt to reverse his position. He will try to go from being on the bottom to being on the top.

One of the easiest ways to go about reversing positions is to use the open or butterfly guard. Optimally, the bottom position fighter will transition to the open guard, and kick back and up into the top fighter's hips while rotating himself. His momentum should topple the top fighter and swing the bottom fighter up on top, possibly into the mount position. We cover that position in Chapter 12.

Take a look at the following photographs and notice how the bottom fighter uses leverage and hip movement to get the reversal.

Reversing from the guard step 1.

(Photo courtesy Mickey Suttiratana)

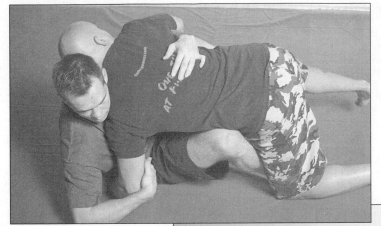

Reversing from the guard step 2.

(Photo courtesy Mickey Suttiratana)

Reversing from the guard step 3.

(Photo courtesy Mickey Suttiratana)

Reversing from the guard step 4.

(Photo courtesy Mickey Suttiratana)

As we've seen, fighters on both the top and bottom have three basic goals while in the guard position. Movement and transitioning are key factors in achieving these goals. If either fighter stops moving while on the ground, it could easily spell defeat for him.

As the fighters jockey for position, both are looking to improve their placement. They're looking for the position that puts them in control. They'll work their way out of the guard position and into the next important groundfighting position: the half guard.

The Least You Need to Know

- The guard is the position most fighters will be in when they take their opponent down to the ground.

- In the guard position, the top and bottom fighters are roughly 50-50 in terms of control.

- The top position fighter looks to ground-and-pound, pass to side control, or gain an unlikely submission.

- The bottom position fighter tries to tie up the fight so they get stood up, get a submission, or reverse his position so he is on top.

Chapter 11

The Half Guard

In This Chapter

- The Half Guard Position
- The Top Position Perspective
- The Bottom Position Perspective

Since the guard is a 50-50 position, if a fighter is not making any headway with his ground-and-pound game, he has two options: back away and allow his opponent to stand up, which he may do anyway if his opponent has a tricky submission game, or attempt to pass guard. He can pass guard from the ground or a standing position … some of that choice is preference. When he attempts to pass guard, he would like to clear the guard to side control or cross mount, but often he will find himself working through the half guard of his opponent. While still not optimal, the half guard does grant the top fighter about 70 to 75 percent control over the fighter on the bottom.

The half guard position represents, as much of what we're covering on the ground does, a transition. Techniques and positions on the ground often occur as the fighters scramble about looking to improve their control. It's important to remember that while the techniques we show in this book appear to happen in linear order, they may not follow suit in an actual competition. Simply put, anything is possible in the chaotic flow of sport combat.

In this chapter, we examine, as we did with the guard in the previous chapter, both the top and bottom perspective in the half guard position.

Being on Top

In the half guard position, the fighter on top has moved most of his body out of the guard position and is attempting to keep as much of his bodyweight on the bottom fighter as possible. The more weight, the less chance the bottom fighter has of moving and improving his position. The top fighter will attempt to keep the bottom fighter flat on his back, while the bottom fighter will try to remain on his side since this will allow him more room to move. The bottom fighter has wrapped his legs around one of the top fighter's legs, however, which is why the half guard does not afford the top fighter complete control. The bottom fighter will also be working for an underhook with the arm opposite the side the top fighter is passing. This is the primary disturbance in the balance of the top fighter, not the legs he has wrapped around his opponent. The underhook is one of the most important jiu-jitsu concepts when you are on the ground.

In both the half guard and the side mount, the real battle is for the single underhook. If the top fighter is able to get it, then he has more control. If the bottom fighter has it, then he has more control. In the Octagon™, it's sometimes difficult to see the battle for this critical position, but you should be alert for it because it enables one of the fighters to better execute the next phase of his strategy.

Working for arm control in the underhook.

(Photo courtesy Mickey Suttiratana)

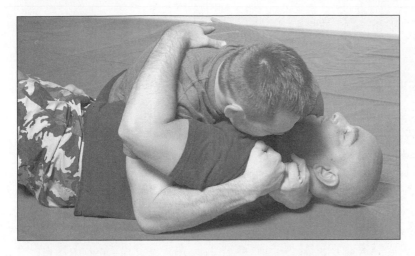

The top fighter gains control in the underhoook.

(Photo courtesy Mickey Suttiratana)

Acquiring the side underhook also enables the top fighter to gain body control over the bottom position fighter as seen in the following photograph.

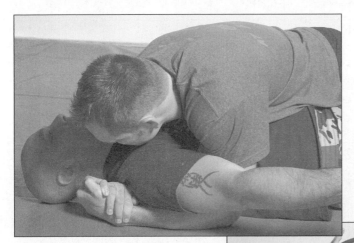

Getting body control in the half guard.

(Photo courtesy Mickey Suttiratana)

Getting body control (reverse angle).

(Photo courtesy Mickey Suttiratana)

At the same time, as we'll see, wrapping both legs around one leg of the top fighter has serious ramifications for the fighter on the bottom.

As before, the fighter on top has several immediate goals: ground-and-pound, submission, or he can look to further improve his position by going to the side mount.

FIGHTER FACTS

Position over submission is a crucial philosophy a lot of fighters embrace. Simply put, it means that a fighter will rarely give up a superior position in order to go after a submission hold, unless the fighter believes he has a high percentage of completing the submission. The strategic advantage of superior position outweighs the possibility that the submission will be successful. This is something to keep in mind when you watch UFC® fights; while you might see a possible submission opportunity, the fighter may not go for it simply because he is in a better position. Also note that there are some low-risk submissions that do not require a fighter to give up his position, and these are attempted frequently, but oftentimes not successfully, because the other fighter may be able to defend them with more ease.

Ground-and-Pound

If the top fighter does not have the opposite side underhook, he will lose his position. As we've stated previously, the quest for the side underhook is therefore paramount. Ground-and-pound is one of the options available to the top fighter in the half guard. For example, top fighters in the half guard may look to use their free leg to unlock the bottom man's legs or for leverage to break the guard and improve to side control. Because the top fighter already has a single underhook on the bottom fighter's other arm, he will look to bring his free arm across and start using elbow strikes to damage his opponent.

The following photos illustrate the positioning necessary to begin inflicting damage with the ground-and-pound strategy from half guard.

Punching in the half guard 1.

(Photo courtesy Mickey Suttiratana)

Punching in the half guard 2.

(Photo courtesy Mickey Suttiratana)

Using elbows in the half guard 1.

(Photo courtesy Mickey Suttiratana)

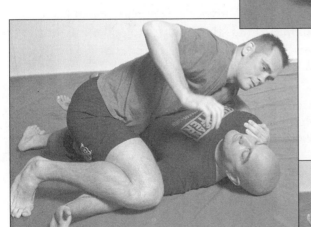

Using elbows in the half guard 2.

(Photo courtesy Mickey Suttiratana)

PRO-FILES | **Rising Star: Joe Stevenson**

(Photo courtesy Zuffa, LLC)

Fighting out of: Las Vegas, Nevada
Born: 6/15/82
Height: 5'7"
Weight: 155 lbs.
Weightclass: Lightweight
Winner of season two of *The Ultimate Fighter*®*; current lightweight contender*

A pro fighter since the age of 16, Joe Stevenson may be the youngest veteran in the sport of mixed martial arts, with close to 40 fights to his name. A ground ace with a deadly guillotine choke, Stevenson defeated Luke Cummo to win the welterweight division of season two of *The Ultimate Fighter*® reality show and then dropped down to his optimum weight of 155 and has since terrorized the lightweight division with wins over Yves Edwards, Dokonjonosuke Mishima and Melvin Guillard.

Submissions

Submissions in the half guard are difficult for the top fighter because one of his legs is trapped by the bottom fighter. The simple truth is that in order to pull off the majority of submission holds, the top fighter needs both of his legs free.

He has only a few options from this position.

Keylock

Watch as the top fighter gets the keylock on the bottom position fighter.

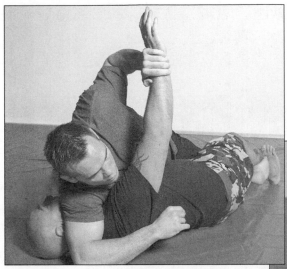

Getting the opponent's arm.

(Photo courtesy Mickey Suttiratana)

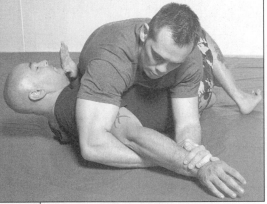

Bringing it to the floor.

(Photo courtesy Mickey Suttiratana)

Bending the arm.

(Photo courtesy Mickey Suttiratana)

Securing the keylock.

(Photo courtesy Mickey Suttiratana)

Here are some alternate views of the keylock.

Working for arm control.
(Photo courtesy Mickey Suttiratana)

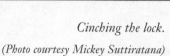

Cinching the lock.
(Photo courtesy Mickey Suttiratana)

Close-up of the keylock.
(Photo courtesy Mickey Suttiratana)

A different angle 1.
(Photo courtesy Mickey Suttiratana)

A different angle 2.
(Photo courtesy Mickey Suttiratana)

Straightened Armbar

The top position fighter also can look to acquire a straightened armbar. The following pictures show this technique in action.

Getting the straightened armbar.

(Photo courtesy Mickey Suttiratana)

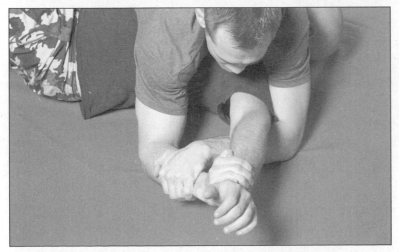

Close-up of the straightened armbar.

(Photo courtesy Mickey Suttiratana)

Arm Triangle

Another option available to the top fighter is the arm triangle. Once the top fighter acquires it, he will then carefully position himself to the other side of the bottom fighter in order to cinch the choke. If the top fighter is not alert, the bottom fighter could reestablish guard. The following pictures show how this works.

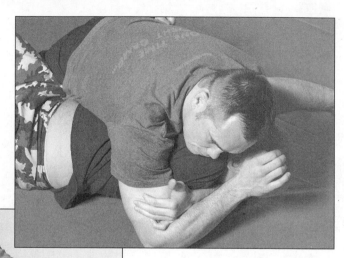

Snaking through for the arm triangle.

(Photo courtesy Mickey Suttiratana)

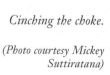

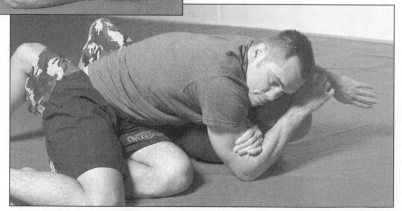

Hopping to the other side.

(Photo courtesy Mickey Suttiratana)

Cinching the choke.

(Photo courtesy Mickey Suttiratana)

It's important to remember that if the top position fighter can get a submission or continue his ground-and-pound game, he most likely will be content to stay in the half guard position. As long as he is racking up damage and points for his work, the top fighter will not be inclined to try to improve his position. As soon as he tries to improve his position, the bottom fighter will furiously attempt to escape.

Improve Position

But if the top position fighter is unable to acquire a submission or the ground-and-pound is ineffective, he will have to try to move into side control, assuming he wants to keep the fight on the ground. This position gives him even more control over the bottom position fighter. It also increases the desperation of the bottom position fighter, who will be more eager to escape and either reestablish the half guard or the guard position, or reverse his position entirely.

On the Bottom

The bottom position fighter in the half guard is not having a good day. His percentage of control has dropped from 50 percent in the guard to just 25 percent. Worse, in order to keep the top fighter from moving into the side mount or mount (which would be virtually catastrophic) the bottom fighter must trap one of the top fighter's legs. In order to do this, the bottom fighter must wrap both of his legs around one of the top fighter's legs. This means that the bottom fighter has very few options available to him. Also note that the bottom fighter never wants to be flat on his back, but must try to remain on a side. Staying on your side allows for more mobility, and makes it difficult for the top fighter to commit to his punches or elbows. He must either improve his position or make a desperate bid for a last-ditch submission hold.

Earning Back the Underhook

It is absolutely critical that the bottom position fighter somehow manage to get the underhook control. If he has any hope of improving his position, this underhook is mandatory. Without it, he has no hope of reversing, standing, or reacquiring the guard.

Reversing Position

If the bottom fighter successfully gets the underhook, he must then look to reverse his position. He does this by kicking his hips up and over. This is illustrated below.

Moving from the half guard.

(Photo courtesy Mickey Suttiratana)

Rolling over.

(Photo courtesy Mickey Suttiratana)

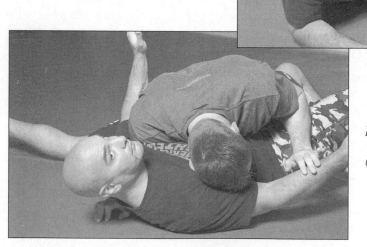

Position reversed.

(Photo courtesy Mickey Suttiratana)

This action may result in several new positions. First, the bottom fighter may "roll" the top fighter onto his back, thereby effectively reversing their positions.

The bottom fighter also may try to reestablish the guard position, at which point things have only improved back to the 50-50 contest. Another way the bottom fighter can take the guard position is to bring his feet up and into the top fighter's back, as if they were in an open guard position, and kick back. The next few photos show this in action.

Starting position for regaining the guard.

(Photo courtesy Mickey Suttiratana)

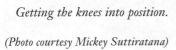

Getting the knees into position.

(Photo courtesy Mickey Suttiratana)

Close-up on knee positioning.

(Photo courtesy Mickey Suttiratana)

The guard is reestablished.

(Photo courtesy Mickey Suttiratana)

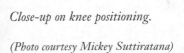
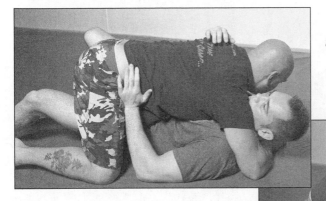

The bottom fighter may escape the half guard and "take the back" if the top fighter stays on his hands and knees. At this point, the bottom fighter becomes the top fighter. The goal then is to dig his heels in (known as "getting his hooks in") to the hips of the bottom fighter, ride him forward to flatten him out and then either punch to the side of the head or go for a rear naked choke.

The next series shows this technique in action.

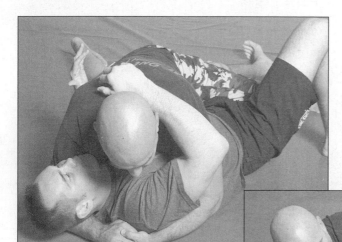

Starting position for the escape.

(Photo courtesy Mickey Suttiratana)

Getting the underhook.

(Photo courtesy Mickey Suttiratana)

Gaining control in the underhook.

(Photo courtesy Mickey Suttiratana)

Starting the roll.

(Photo courtesy Mickey Suttiratana)

Continuing the roll.

(Photo courtesy Mickey Suttiratana)

Taking the back.

(Photo courtesy Mickey Suttiratana)

Digging the hooks in.

(Photo courtesy Mickey Suttiratana)

The top fighter, for his part, will try to counter the counter by pulling off an "anaconda" choke, snaking his arms around the neck of the bottom fighter and pressing down on his head to compress the airway and blood vessels. This is an advanced choke, but extremely effective.

Another option for the bottom fighter is a takedown. As the bottom fighter rolls the top fighter off of him, the top fighter may start to stand. At this point, the bottom fighter may attempt either a single or double leg takedown and then reestablish the guard. Although many fighters end up in guard off their takedown attempts, it would be optimal to put yourself in a better position such as cross mount.

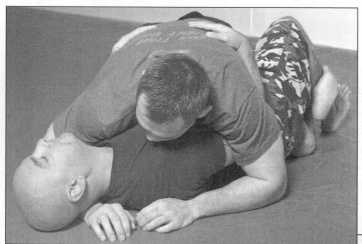

Start position for the anaconda choke.

(Photo courtesy Mickey Suttiratana)

Pressing the head down toward the waist.

(Photo courtesy Mickey Suttiratana)

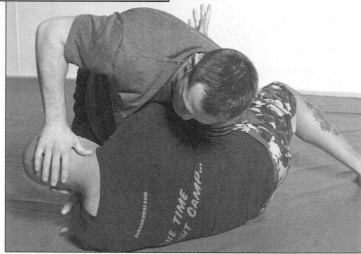

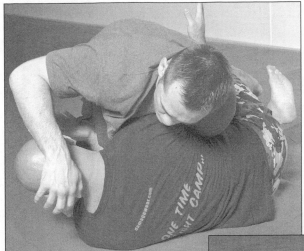

Close-up.

(Photo courtesy Mickey Suttiratana)

*Snaking the hand up and through
for the choke.*

(Photo courtesy Mickey Suttiratana)

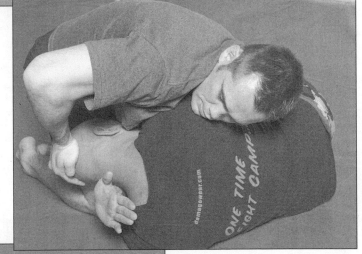

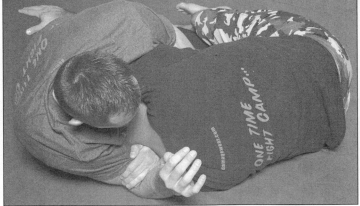

Cinching the choke.

(Photo courtesy Mickey Suttiratana)

UFC LEGENDS | **Mark Coleman**

(Photo courtesy Zuffa, LLC)

Fought out of: Columbus, Ohio
Born: 12/20/64
Height: 6'1"
Weight: 245 lbs.
Weightclass: Heavyweight
First UFC Heavyweight Champion; two-time UFC Tournament Champion

As the UFC's first heavyweight champion, Mark "The Hammer" Coleman has stood face-to-face and persevered over opponents like Gary Goodridge and Don Frye. But his biggest surge in popularity came when he choked out UFC sensation Dan Severn at 2:47 in the first round at UFC 12, claiming the heavyweight title in the process. Always a crowd favorite for his thunderous slams and devastating ground-and-pound attack, Coleman left the UFC with a record of 6-3 in 1999 after losing his last three bouts in the Octagon.

Last-Ditch Submissions

If the quest to improve his position does not seem to be working, the bottom fighter may look for a chance to get a submission hold on the top fighter.

This is extremely difficult to do since most of the seasoned fighters in the UFC know exactly what the bottom fighter will be looking for. They therefore know how to avoid falling into the trap.

However, as we've mentioned before, the chaos of a fight combined with the stress and exhaustion of constant struggle may make the top fighter momentarily lose his awareness. If the bottom fighter is sharp, that will be the moment he springs the trap.

With limited submission holds available to him, the bottom fighter absolutely must be fighting to get out of the half guard position. He either has to look to reestablish the guard or else reverse his position.

If he does not, the top fighter will either win with a ground-and-pound or a submission, or he will improve to the side control. In any event, the bottom fighter loses.

The half guard represents a turning point in the battle. No longer is the contest on the ground a 50-50 match of wills. The half guard gives a decided advantage to the top fighter, who will look for a ground-and-pound, a submission, or to improve his position even further.

For the fighter on the bottom, the bout has gone bad and he must rapidly take steps to correct his course. He has severely limited submissions available. By far his most pressing need is to get out of the half guard.

Notable Fights

Hominick vs. Edwards at UFC 58.

(Photo courtesy Zuffa, LLC)

March 4, 2006: Mandalay Bay Events Center, Las Vegas, Nevada

Lightweights Mark Hominick and Yves Edwards opened up the action at *UFC 58: USA vs. Canada* and expectations were high for Edwards, a top contender for years, to take the upstart Hominick easily.

In the first round, both fighters launched volley after volley of strikes, but nothing seemed to land well enough to damage the other fighter. And as visually appealing as the strikes might have been, there was little that marked the round as significant, including an absolute lack of any groundfighting.

In round two, however, Hominick nailed Edwards with a series of hard body shots. Edwards clinched and took Hominick down to the ground. Hominick, on his back, began working for the triangle armbar and after a minute or so of trying, finally cinched it down. Edwards was forced to tap out at 1:52 of the second round in one of the big upsets of 2006.

The Least You Need to Know

◆ The half guard position gives 70 to 75 percent control to the fighter on top.

◆ The top fighter can ground-and-pound, look for limited submissions, or improve his position to side control.

◆ The fighter on the bottom must either use a last-ditch submission hold or get out of the half guard.

◆ The bottom position fighter can revert to the guard, or look to reverse his position by kicking up with his hips.

◆ As the bottom fighter tries to reverse his position, the top fighter can "counter the counter" with any number of transitional positions.

The Side Mount

In This Chapter

◆ The Side Control Position

◆ The Top Position Perspective

◆ The Bottom Position Perspective

The ground war is heating up. The top fighter has now moved from the half guard position into the side control. In this position, the advantage swings even more to the top position fighter, assuming he has already achieved and maintained the underhook. If he has not gotten the underhook, as he tries to transition to side control, he will lose position. For the bottom fighter, things are now desperate. But even in this position, the bottom fighter may still be able to survive. Chief among them is to earn the underhook for himself and get an escape from his position.

In this chapter, we'll look at the side control position, again from the perspectives of the fighter on top and the fighter on the bottom. As with the chapter on the half guard, please be aware that many of the positions that are illustrated happen off of transitions and are not limited to the pictorial flow in which they appear.

Being on Top

The top fighter has improved his position to the side mount. Things are now looking pretty good indeed.

With both of his legs free, the top fighter now has a wide range of things he can look to do from this position to end the fight. He can again launch a ground-and-pound attack. He can look for a variety of submission holds. Or he can look to again improve his position and acquire the dreaded mount. He will need the opposite side underhook to maintain his position. When the top fighter is striking, he must not give up too much space to the bottom fighter enabling him to regain the underhook. If so, the bottom fighter has greatly increased his chance of escaping the side mount. Also, bear in mind that some fighters prefer to do their ground-and-pound from the cross mount and not the mount.

Ground-and-Pound

In side control, there is still a constant battle for the side underhook. The top position fighter may look to trap the other arm with one of his knees and then punch or elbow the face of the opponent. Knee strikes are unlikely in this position simply because as the top fighter rears back to strike with the knee, it will give enough space to the bottom fighter to escape the trapped arm.

PRO-FILES   **Rising Star: Kendall Grove**

(Photo courtesy Zuffa, LLC)

Fighting out of: Maui, Hawaii
Born: 11/12/82
Height: 6'6"
Weight: 185 lbs.
Weightclass: Middleweight
Middleweight winner of season three of *The Ultimate Fighter®*

A huge middleweight at 6 foot 6, Kendall "Da Spyder" Grove is a star on the rise whose development as a fighter was shown on national television during his stint on *The Ultimate Fighter®* reality series. A training partner of former UFC® champion Tito Ortiz, who coached Grove on the show, Kendall won the series title with a stirring three-round win over Ed Herman, and has continued to improve with each successive victory.

Submissions

Because the top position fighter now has both of his legs free, he is in a much better position to get submissions. We'll look at some of the more common submissions available in the following photographs.

Straight Armbar

The most common submission is the straightened armbar. The top fighter will attempt to gain leverage on the arm and hyperextend the elbow joint for the submission.

Starting the straightened armbar.

(Photo courtesy Mickey Suttiratana)

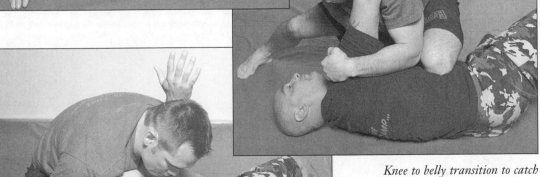

Knee to belly transition to catch the arm.

(Photo courtesy Mickey Suttiratana)

Starting to spin.

(Photo courtesy Mickey Suttiratana)

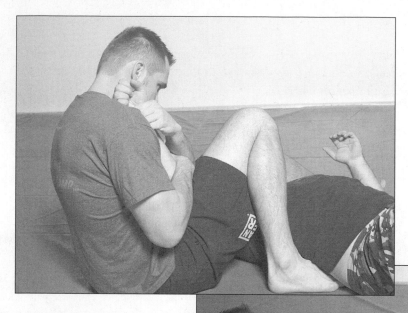

Catching the arm and leaning back.

(Photo courtesy Mickey Suttiratana)

Leaning back with the arm fully extended.

(Photo courtesy Mickey Suttiratana)

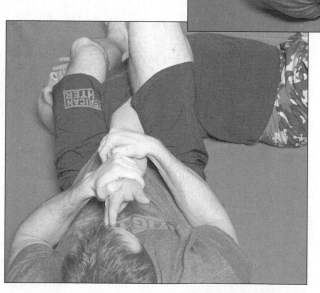

Reverse angle on a completed lock.

(Photo courtesy Mickey Suttiratana)

Rich Franklin delivers a knockout blow to Nate Quarry at UFC 56.

(Photo courtesy Zuffa, LLC)

Rashad Evans mitigates the 50 pound weight advantage of his opponent, Brad Imes, at The Ultimate Fighter 2 Finale.

(Photo courtesy Zuffa, LLC)

Matt Hughes with one of his signature throws at UFC 36.

(Photo courtesy Zuffa, LLC)

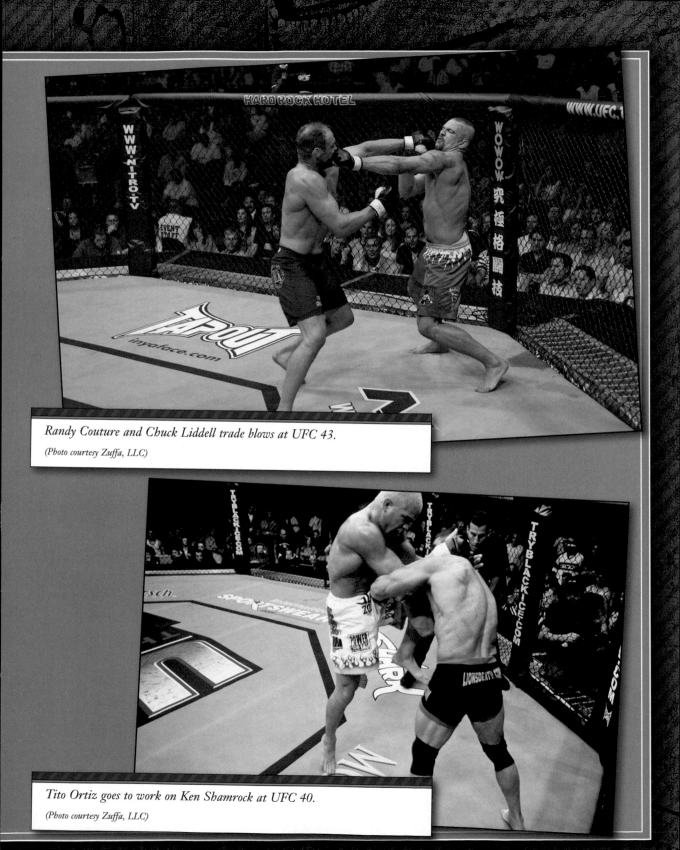

Randy Couture and Chuck Liddell trade blows at UFC 43.

(Photo courtesy Zuffa, LLC)

Tito Ortiz goes to work on Ken Shamrock at UFC 40.

(Photo courtesy Zuffa, LLC)

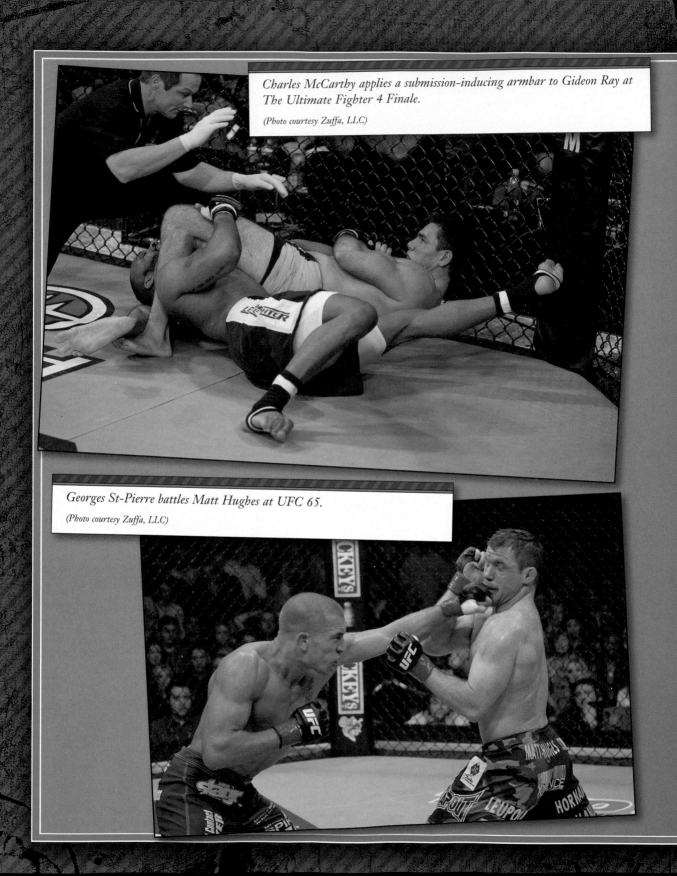

Charles McCarthy applies a submission-inducing armbar to Gideon Ray at The Ultimate Fighter 4 Finale.

(Photo courtesy Zuffa, LLC)

Georges St-Pierre battles Matt Hughes at UFC 65.

(Photo courtesy Zuffa, LLC)

*Rich Franklin uses his athleticism to score a takedown against David
Loiseau at UFC 58.*

(Photo courtesy Zuffa, LLC)

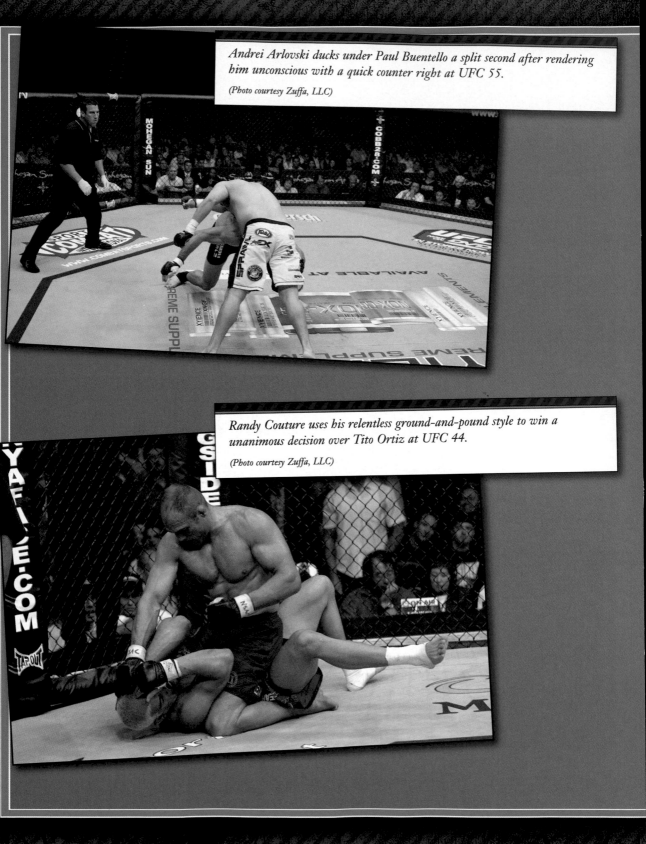

Andrei Arlovski ducks under Paul Buentello a split second after rendering him unconscious with a quick counter right at UFC 55.

(Photo courtesy Zuffa, LLC)

Randy Couture uses his relentless ground-and-pound style to win a unanimous decision over Tito Ortiz at UFC 44.

(Photo courtesy Zuffa, LLC)

Forrest Griffin gets the better of Stephan Bonnar during their rematch at UFC 62.

(Photo courtesy Zuffa, LLC)

Dean Lister wraps up Yuki Sasaki at UFC Fight Night 6.

(Photo courtesy Zuffa, LLC)

Kendall Grove and Ed Herman put on a nonstop action-packed performance at The Ultimate Fighter 3 Finale.

(Photo courtesy Zuffa, LLC)

Rich Franklin attacks Evan Tanner with a flying knee during their rematch at UFC 53. With the round 4 TKO victory, Franklin became the UFC Middleweight Champion.

(Photo courtesy Zuffa, LLC)

Choke

The top position fighter can look to clear the bottom fighter's arm and acquire a choke. The picture series below illustrates this.

Clearing the arm.

(Photo courtesy Mickey Suttiratana)

Snaking the hand through.

(Photo courtesy Mickey Suttiratana)

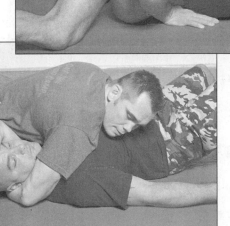

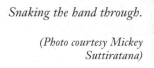

Cinching the choke.

(Photo courtesy Mickey Suttiratana)

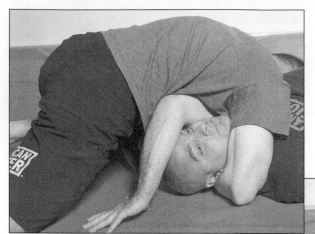

Close-up on the choke.

(Photo courtesy Mickey Suttiratana)

Reverse angle on the choke.

(Photo courtesy Mickey Suttiratana)

Change Position to North-South

The top position fighter may want to move into a north-south position. This is basically still a side mount, but it enables the top fighter to work chokes as he swings into north-south. The top fighter will also look to isolate the arm, inflict ground-and-pound, and then move into more chokes.

The north-south position.

(Photo courtesy Mickey Suttiratana)

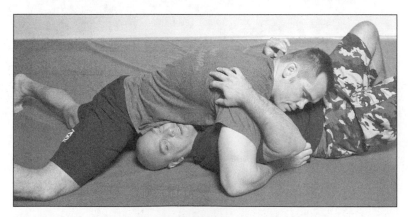

Armbar

The top fighter in the north-south position might try to isolate an arm, spin, and get an armbar. These pictures show how this is accomplished.

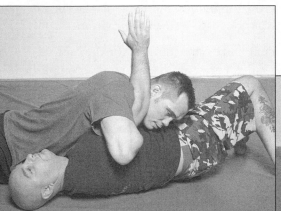

Starting the armbar.

(Photo courtesy Mickey Suttiratana)

Coming up to start the spin.

(Photo courtesy Mickey Suttiratana)

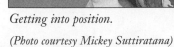

Getting into position.

(Photo courtesy Mickey Suttiratana)

Starting to lean back.

(Photo courtesy Mickey Suttiratana)

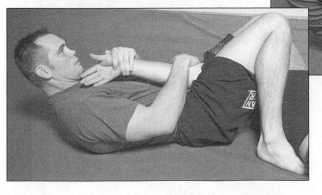

Leaning back with arm fully extended.

(Photo courtesy Mickey Suttiratana)

Improve Position

The last option for top position fighters in the side mount is to improve their position to the mount. Some fighters do not view this as an improvement. At this point, however, the side mount offers a great deal to the top fighter and they may not be inclined to move into a new position, unless they can adequately cover their advance.

The key throughout any movement is to minimize opportunities for the bottom fighter to improve his position through counters or reversals, which is accomplished by minimizing the amount of space you give him.

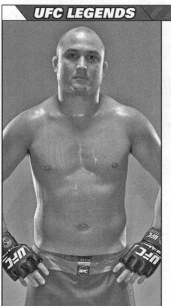

UFC LEGENDS **BJ Penn**

(Photo courtesy Zuffa, LLC)

Fighting out of: Hilo, Hawaii
Born: 12/13/78
Height: 5'9"
Weight: 155–170 lbs.
Weightclass: Lightweight-Welterweight
Former UFC Welterweight Champion, coach on season five of *The Ultimate Fighter*®

A fighter whose talent earned him the moniker "The Prodigy," BJ Penn has fought and beaten the best in the world since his highly anticipated MMA debut in 2001. Best remembered for his shocking submission win over Matt Hughes in his welterweight debut in 2004, after a successful run at lightweight. Penn returned to 155 pounds to take on the last man who beat him in that weight class, his fellow coach on the fifth season of *The Ultimate Fighter*®, Jens Pulver.

On the Bottom

It's not good being on the bottom in the side mount. That's the simple truth. The situation has gone from bad in the half guard to worse in the side mount. And unless the bottom fighter is able to get moving, the fight most likely will be over soon.

There is really only one option on the bottom: reestablish some type of position that at least gives more control than the very little he has in the side mount.

Reversal of Fortune

The key to the bottom fighter's survival at this point is the side underhook. He must get this underhook in order to give himself the necessary leverage to reverse his position.

Assuming the bottom fighter gets this underhook, the next moves he makes will be the same as the moves he made to reverse himself in the half guard. He will kick his hips up and over, rolling the top fighter.

This photo series shows a typical reversal.

Top fighter is rolled as the bottom fighter starts the reversal.

(Photo courtesy Mickey Suttiratana)

Realizing he is losing his position, the top fighter fights to retain the guard.

(Photo courtesy Mickey Suttiratana)

Control in the guard with positions reversed.

(Photo courtesy Mickey Suttiratana)

While the bottom fighter will look to obtain side control, once the top fighter realizes he is losing the position, he will fight to retain it. But if he senses that fighting for it may not work to his advantage, he most likely will go back to the guard and start working from there again, or he could give up position and stand up if he does not want to be on bottom.

North-South Belly-Down

Another option the top fighter has is to move into a north-south belly-down position as the bottom fighter reverses, especially if the top fighter is a good wrestler. Please note that this usually occurs during a scramble for position.

FIGHTER FACTS

This is a perfect example of how style types come into play. When Jiu-Jitsu stylists realize they're losing position, they will roll and reestablish the guard. But a wrestling stylist will fight the bottom fighter every inch of the way.

Stuffing the Reversal

In the following pictures, the bottom fighter reverses and the top fighter "stuffs" the reversal and moves into north-south belly-down.

The bottom fighter attempts to reverse.

(Photo courtesy Mickey Suttiratana)

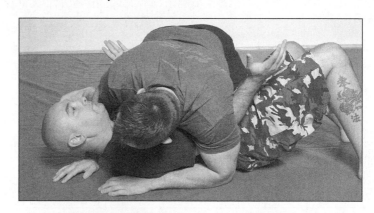

As he rolls, the top fighter moves with him.

(Photo courtesy Mickey Suttiratana)

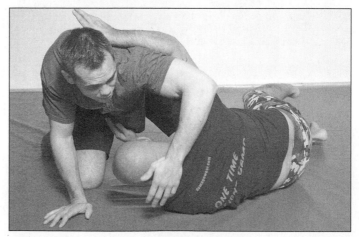

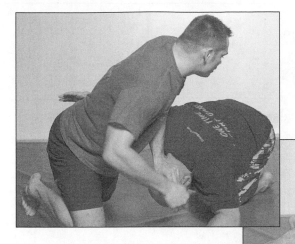

The top fighter transitions to north-south belly-down …

(Photo courtesy Mickey Suttiratana)

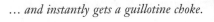

… and instantly gets a guillotine choke.

(Photo courtesy Mickey Suttiratana)

For the fighter on the bottom during a north-south transition, he must get out quickly before the top fighter has a chance to cinch down a choke or inflict too much damage with the ground-and-pound.

Looking for the choke from the north-south belly-down.

(Photo courtesy Mickey Suttiratana)

Snaking arm through.

(Photo courtesy Mickey Suttiratana)

Pressing the head down.

(Photo courtesy Mickey Suttiratana)

Cinching the choke.

(Photo courtesy Mickey Suttiratana)

Starting to roll over.

(Photo courtesy Mickey Suttiratana)

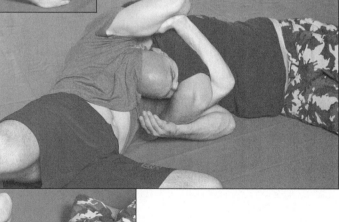

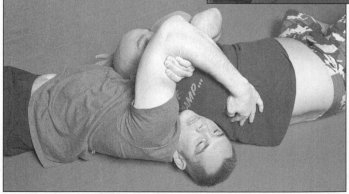

The front choke on fully.

(Photo courtesy Mickey Suttiratana)

Taking the Back

If the bottom fighter uses the underhook to leverage himself into a takedown, normally one of two things will happen: The top fighter will roll, doing his best to establish guard once he finds himself off-balance. Or the top fighter will try to flee, usually ending in a situation fighting a single or double leg.

However, it is possible for the bottom fighter to take the back of the top fighter if the top fighter is caught unaware as the bottom fighter begins to leverage his underhook and bump his hips.

At this point, the fighter on the back will look to get his hooks in, then flatten the fighter on the bottom. If the top fighter doesn't flatten the bottom fighter, the bottom guy can roll and keep the top man off-balance.

Once the bottom fighter is flattened, he has no options. Meanwhile, the top fighter can look to impose a serious ground-and-pound attack. The top fighter also can look to get a rear naked choke, especially building into it off the ground-and-pound.

This series of photos shows some of the options available once the fighter has taken the back from the north-south position.

Starting position from north-south belly-down.

(Photo courtesy Mickey Suttiratana)

Moving around.

(Photo courtesy Mickey Suttiratana)

Taking the back.

(Photo courtesy Mickey Suttiratana)

Digging in the hooks.

(Photo courtesy Mickey Suttiratana)

Close-up on feet position.

(Photo courtesy Mickey Suttiratana)

Flattening the bottom fighter.

(Photo courtesy Mickey Suttiratana)

Ground-and-pound with elbow strikes ...

(Photo courtesy Mickey Suttiratana)

... or punches.

(Photo courtesy Mickey Suttiratana)

The rear naked choke.

(Photo courtesy Mickey Suttiratana)

The following pictures show an escape from the side mount to take the back.

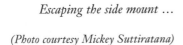

Escaping the side mount ...

(Photo courtesy Mickey Suttiratana)

... and moving in to take the back.

(Photo courtesy Mickey Suttiratana)

Notable Fights

Lauzon vs. Pulver at UFC 63.

(Photo courtesy Zuffa, LLC)

September 23, 2006: Arrowhead Pond, Anaheim, CA

With fans and experts alike expecting to see a dramatic return for former UFC Lightweight Champion Jens Pulver at UFC 63, no one could have predicted what would befall the crowd favorite when he stepped into the Octagon™ that night.

As soon as the fight started, the unheralded Joe Lauzon shot for a takedown and got it, shoving Pulver into the cage. Lauzon attempted to unleash a bit of ground-and-pound action, but Pulver fought his way out of the situation and returned to his feet.

Pulver then attempted a punch, but his feet weren't quite under him. He slipped and ran into a barrage of strikes from Lauzon. Lauzon followed with a knee and then came over the top with a left that floored Pulver.

As soon as Pulver was down, Lauzon unleashed a volley of hits that prompted the referee to step in and end the fight. The upstart Lauzon demolished Pulver, shocking everyone in the mixed martial arts world.

In the side mount, the fight really belongs to the fighter on top, so long as he has the underhook. He has the ability to ground-and-pound, isolate arms, get chokes, apply knee strikes with the leg closest to his opponent's hip, transition into other positions like the north-south, or switch to the full mount.

For the fighter on the bottom, time is running out. He must get a reversal or at least improve back to half guard or, preferably, the guard. If he is unable to do this, the chances are high that he will lose the fight.

The Least You Need to Know

◆ The side control grants almost total domination to the fighter on top, provided he can acquire and maintain the underhook.

◆ The top fighter can ground-and-pound, look for submissions, change position, or optimally, improve his position. Again, improvement is a preference.

◆ The bottom fighter has no significant submissions available and must try to reverse or better his position through the acquisition of the underhook.

Chapter 13

The Mount

In This Chapter

- ◆ The Mount
- ◆ The Top Position Perspective
- ◆ The Bottom Position Perspective

If the top position fighter has decided to change to the full mount position, he is now in almost complete control of the fight. As we see in this chapter, the fight is almost his to lose at this point.

For the fighter on the bottom, the situation is grave. His options are extremely limited; he has only one choice: get out of the position he is in. It's the only way he will survive and get himself another shot at victory.

In this chapter, we look at how the top and bottom fighters deal with being in the mount.

It's Great Being on Top

As we mentioned, the top position fighter in the mount is in an almost totally dominant position over his opponent.

The mount.

(Photo courtesy Mickey Suttiratana)

The fighter on top has several choices open, but more than any other, he will look to end the fight quickly using the option that causes the most damage in the least amount of time.

Ground-and-Pound

The easiest avenue of attack after obtaining the mount is striking. The top position fighter has both arms available and can literally rain down punches and elbows on his opponent's head and face. The damage builds up startlingly fast and more often than not, the referee will stop the fight soon after it starts—especially if the bottom fighter seems unable to defend himself. Striking might also conceivably cause the bottom fighter to turn and give up his back, which would be a horrible and unlikely mistake.

The following pictures show the ground-and-pound in action.

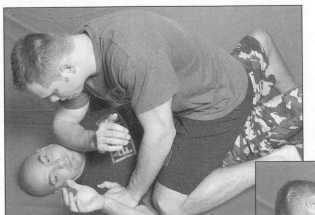

Elbow strikes from the mount.

(Photo courtesy Mickey Suttiratana)

Punching from the mount.

(Photo courtesy Mickey Suttiratana)

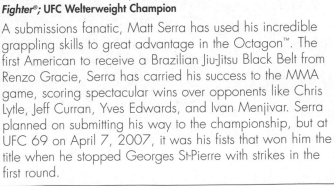

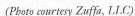
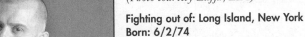
PRO-FILES   *Rising Star: Matt "The Terror" Serra*

(Photo courtesy Zuffa, LLC)

Fighting out of: Long Island, New York
Born: 6/2/74
Height: 5'6"
Weight: 170 lbs.
Weightclass: Welterweight
Brazilian Jiu-Jitsu Black Belt, winner of season four of *The Ultimate Fighter*®**; UFC Welterweight Champion**

A submissions fanatic, Matt Serra has used his incredible grappling skills to great advantage in the Octagon™. The first American to receive a Brazilian Jiu-Jitsu Black Belt from Renzo Gracie, Serra has carried his success to the MMA game, scoring spectacular wins over opponents like Chris Lytle, Jeff Curran, Yves Edwards, and Ivan Menjivar. Serra planned on submitting his way to the championship, but at UFC 69 on April 7, 2007, it was his fists that won him the title when he stopped Georges St-Pierre with strikes in the first round.

Submissions

The top position fighter also can try for a submission from the mount, but he will usually only do so if the bottom fighter is trying to ward off his punches and extends an arm too much, or if he is otherwise lazy.

Armbars

The following photos show several examples of armbars from the mount position.

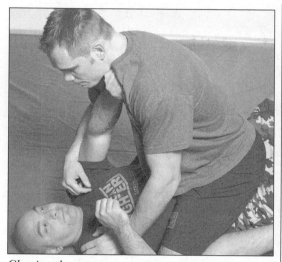

Clearing the arm.

(Photo courtesy Mickey Suttiratana)

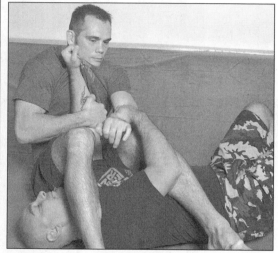

Starting to lean back with the armbar.

(Photo courtesy Mickey Suttiratana)

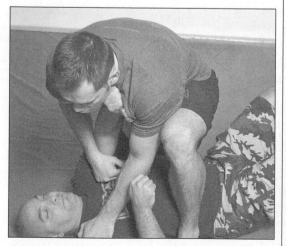

Starting the spin.

(Photo courtesy Mickey Suttiratana)

Completed armbar.

(Photo courtesy Mickey Suttiratana)

Chokes

The top fighter may look for an arm triangle choke, although this is a bit tricky to pull off in the mount. In order to fully execute an effective choke, therefore, the top fighter will dismount into a side control, which allows for maximum pressure and a possible tap-out from the opponent.

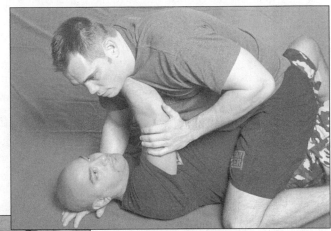

Clearing the arm.

(Photo courtesy Mickey Suttiratana)

Cinching the choke.

(Photo courtesy Mickey Suttiratana)

Preparing to move to the side mount to complete the choke.

(Photo courtesy Mickey Suttiratana)

While it's vital to remember that most fighters will not go for a submission over a position, savvy vets will always take advantage of an opportunity if they believe they have a high probability of success. This might include changing position (knee on belly) or attempting a submission.

The mount basically concludes the ground war for the top fighter. He should be able to finish off his opponent easily from this position.

On the Bottom

Desperation marks the attitude of the bottom fighter in the mount. He must get out of the position immediately. Punches are already on their way.

The one thing the bottom fighter can use to his advantage from the mount is the lack of stability that the top fighter has. In the side mount, the top fighter has better stability, but can only hit with one arm. In the mount, the top fighter has less stability, but can hit with both arms. It's a trade-off, and if the bottom fighter is alert, he can use this lack of balance to his benefit.

UFC LEGENDS   *Andrei Arlovski*

(Photo courtesy Zuffa, LLC)

Fighting out of: Chicago, Illinois, by way of Minsk, Belarus
Born: 2/4/79
Height: 6'3"
Weight: 240 lbs.
Weightclass: Heavyweight
Former UFC® Heavyweight Champion

Known as "The Pitbull" for his tenacious attacks in the Octagon, Andrei Arlovski is one of the most dangerous fighters in mixed martial arts today, not only because of his fight-ending power, but for his impressive ground game. The former UFC Heavyweight Champion holds a first-round submission win over Tim Sylvia and also notched two successful title defenses. Arlovski is currently on the comeback trail after losing his belt to Sylvia, and he has his sights on once again reigning atop the division.

Getting Out

The key to all mount escapes is controlling the top fighter's base (hips). The bottom fighter will push and create space with his hands or use his hips to buck the top fighter. If he is able to create that space, his chances of escape improve.

Regaining the Guard

The following photos show how the bottom fighter can work to regain the guard.

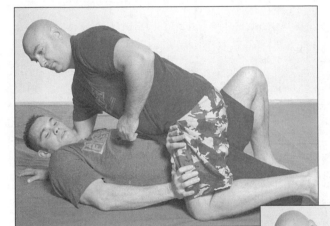

*Using the hands to push back
against top fighter's hips.*

(Photo courtesy Mickey Suttiratana)

Bringing the legs up.

(Photo courtesy Mickey Suttiratana)

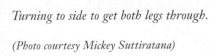

Turning to side to get both legs through.

(Photo courtesy Mickey Suttiratana)

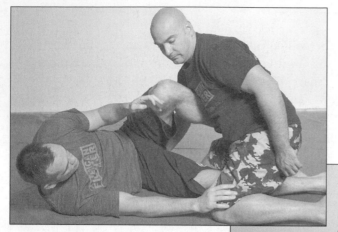

Bringing one leg to the outside.

(Photo courtesy Mickey Suttiratana)

*Getting the other leg outside
to regain the guard.*

(Photo courtesy Mickey Suttiratana)

Reversal

The following series demonstrate how to reverse positions from the bottom of the mount.

While the submissions may look different over the course of the ground war, they are in effect the same submissions from chapter to chapter. They appear different because they are being executed from different positions on the ground.

And while there are indeed more advanced chokes and submission holds, our goal is to show you the basic and effective holds that will be seen in almost every UFC bout.

Remember that chokes, submissions, and reversals tend to happen during transitions to different positions, or in the midst of a break in the action. Each fighter, whether on top or the bottom, is looking for the chance to swing the battle in his favor—to secure the win.

Starting the reversal.

(Photo courtesy Mickey Suttiratana)

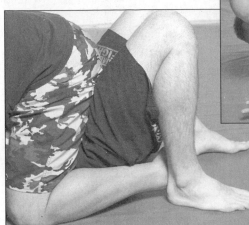

Close-up on feet position.

(Photo courtesy Mickey Suttiratana)

Kicking up with hips to off-balance top fighter.

(Photo courtesy Mickey Suttiratana)

Continuing the roll.

(Photo courtesy Mickey Suttiratana)

Positions reversed, in guard.

(Photo courtesy Mickey Suttiratana)

Notable Fights

Franca vs. Varner at UFC 62

(Photo courtesy Zuffa, LLC)

August 26, 2006: Mandalay Bay Events Center, Las Vegas, NV

Hermes Franca squared off against Jamie Varner in this lightweight division fight at UFC 62. In the first round, both men scored well with standup strikes and also engaged in some ground action.

Varner seemed more aggressive than Franca, but round one wasn't decisive for either fighter. Franca spent the majority of the time on his back and Varner tried unsuccessfully to work both in his guard and standing up. Toward the end of round one, Franca managed to land a good kick and a right punch.

In round two, Franca came out with a kick and Varner took him to the ground again. He worked in Franca's guard, trying to rain down punches, but Franca protected himself incredibly well. Varner moved to half guard and the pair were then stood up because things were not progressing.

Varner again got Franca on the ground and after a number of reversals, Franca got on top of Varner. He went for a triangle choke but Varner was able to throw Franca off his back. Varner took Franca down again, but was unable to do anything of substance.

In round three, Franca's aggression was evident, as he looked to pull away in what had been a very close fight. Varner was able to thwart most of his attacks and went for another takedown. This time Franca dodged. Varner shot again and took a hard knee to his face. He was clearly shaken and retreated. He lost his mouthpiece and a point from the referee. Franca saw an opportunity and attacked with his knees. Varner finally got a takedown, but Franca was able to get on top. He stood and Varner got yet another takedown. This time, Franca was able to secure a deep armbar and Varner was forced to tap out at 3:31 in round three.

The Least You Need to Know

- The mount grants virtually total dominance to the top fighter.

- The top fighter will look to end the fight with a ground-and-pound from the mount.

- The top position fighter does have submission options, but is unlikely to sacrifice his position for a submission unless he is confident in his submission prowess.

- The bottom position fighter must get out of the mount or else he will lose the match. Even if he avoids submissions and the barrage of ground-and-pound, he will lose on points.

- In order to escape from the mount, the bottom fighter must use his hands to control the top fighter's hips and create space.

Part 5

What It Takes to Be an Ultimate Fighter™ Athlete

By the time a UFC® fighter makes his way into the Octagon™, he may have spent months preparing for the bout. Long hours of training, exhausting drills, working with coaches and managers, and developing strategy all go into the grueling preparations that every fighter undergoes. In this part, we take a look inside the process of getting ready to enter the Octagon.

Chapter 14

Fight-Specific Training

In This Chapter

- ◆ Sizing Up the Other Guy
- ◆ Building a Game Plan
- ◆ Finding the Right Help
- ◆ Sparring

While we've covered the techniques and stages of an actual fight, there is a whole lot more that goes into the preparation for a bout in the Octagon™. Fighters not only need to know how to punch, kick, clinch, and takedown, they also need the assistance of an array of competent professionals to help make sure they are doing all the right things as they train for their next fight.

In this chapter, we take an insider's look at just how today's UFC® fighters go about gearing up for a fight. We examine the ways they size up their opponents, how they develop strategies for dealing with him, and how a fighter puts together his team of trainers and sparring partners so he has the best possible chance of success.

It's not all about fighting in the cage itself. There's a lot of work that needs to be done before the fighter even steps into the infamous Octagon.

Sizing Up the Competition

When a fight is announced, the first thing each fighter wants to do is examine their competition in detail. With an analysis that would make the Central Intelligence Agency proud, fighters and their team pore over records, fight tapes, and any other information they can glean to help build a comprehensive picture of the man they'll soon face.

Tapes

Perhaps more vital than any other piece of information, a fighter's team will pull tapes of all the competitor's recent bouts, as well as a few older bouts. They will watch the tapes over and over, stopping or pausing to learn how their opponent fights. Every detail will be examined, from how he holds his hands, to how he leads during a kick, and how he slips his strikes in during a clinch. What holds does he favor? Where does he seem weakest as he moves in to launch a technique?

Along with this assessment, the fighter's team is comparing how the opponent fights to how their man fights. Does the opponent have any visible weakness that can be exploited? Does he seem to have a weak chin that might mean he can be taken out with a good punch? What is his takedown defense like? If he's a fighter who favors wrestling moves, does his standup suffer as a result?

These and many more questions will be asked during the tape review. As answers suggest themselves, the team formulates a good picture of just what their man is going to have to do to win over his opponent.

FIGHTER FACTS

Depending on the opponent, reviewing tapes can take quite a while. Some fighters have records with well over two dozen matches. If these have been recorded, a fighter's team may want to look at all of them. Each tape is studied carefully—sometimes progressing slowly ahead frame-by-frame—and depending on when the fight was fought, can reveal amazing insights into the opponent. These insights help the fighter in his preparation by getting him ready for as many scenarios as possible—although all fighters realize that the opponent on the tape may not be the opponent who shows up to their match.

Training

Along with tapes, the fighter's team will want to know who the opponent is training with. This is valuable intelligence that will be used to help build a game plan. If the opponent is studying with a famed wrestling technique coach, does that mean he might haul those skills out during a fight? If he's working kicking down walls, will he be looking to use his legs to score a knockout?

Along with finding out who he's training with, the fighter's team will want to know how he trains. Does he go all day or are there too many rest periods built into his schedule? Does he seem determined to win, or is some of that all-important spirit lacking? What about endurance training? Does he do enough roadwork to stay active for five five-minute rounds? Can he keep up?

Personal Life

While some experts would not choose to focus on this area as much, there's little doubt that a fighter's personal life can affect how they approach a fight. If there's a great deal of stress or anxiety in the opponent's personal life, there may be a chance it will spill over into even the most disciplined of fighters. As such, a previously unshakable fighter may be compromised.

With all these factors now resolved, the fighter's team looks to the next stage of preparation …

Building a Game Plan

With the valuable intelligence gleaned from fight tapes, training camp reports, and insight into the opponent's personal life, the fighter's team is now able to build a game plan. This is the basic strategy the fighter will use to try to defeat his opponent.

Most fighters will look at the information and attempt to reason out what the "worst-case scenario" might be in the course of the fight. They will then specifically train for this scenario in the event it comes up.

For example, if the opponent is a gifted Muay Thai stylist renowned for his use of the clinch to deliver an awesome barrage of knee strikes, then the fighter will train to defend himself against such attacks. By constantly putting himself on the receiving end during practice, he will gain confidence in dealing with that situation. Hopefully, it will keep him protected during the fight, forcing the opponent to abandon or at least temporarily sideline that particular weapon and try something else. If the fighter can keep his opponent off his game, constantly having to try other tactics, then the fighter has a much better chance of winning.

At the same time, the fighter will focus on training his own strengths, and improving areas that might be weaker than others. The fighter stacks his strengths against the strengths of his opponent and develops a road map to winning the fight.

Once he has this basic guideline, he must start his training. And for that, he needs the very best help he can afford to bring to his team.

PRO-FILES | **Rising Star: Hermes Franca**

(Photo courtesy Zuffa, LLC)

Fighting out of: Jupiter, Florida
Born: 8/27/74
Height: 5'6"
Weight: 155 lbs.
Weightclass: Lightweight
Brazilian Jiu-Jitsu Black Belt

Hermes Franca knows what it's like to lose. After three losses in 2005, Franca was considered an endangered species by a lot of fans and experts. But Franca kept working, refocused himself, and he has put together a series of impressive victories. With a fantastic ground game and a smorgasbord of submissions up his sleeve, as well as an underrated striking game, Franca has the type of well-rounded game that is essential for success in the stacked UFC lightweight division.

It's All About the Help

Since mixed martial arts covers the entire spectrum of striking and grappling, today's UFC gladiators need to make sure that they are constantly training in these areas to improve their game. At no time does this become more crucial than in the months and weeks leading up to a fight.

While some fighters have access to different teachers and coaches in the same facility, other fighters travel to different schools for their training. A fighter might take classes at a Jiu-Jitsu school to work on his chokes and ground game. He might have a wrestling coach tutor him on takedowns and slams, as well as different tactics in the clinch. And he might work out at a number of places that will help his standup striking game excel—such as boxing and Muay Thai academies.

A fighter will generally have specific areas to work on within each of these disciplines. He may want to work on his right cross at the boxing gym. He may want to improve his knee strikes at the Muay Thai school. If his guillotine choke seems inadequate, he may want to practice that at the Jiu-Jitsu academy.

Obviously, all this training takes scheduling to a whole new level. It's not uncommon for fighters to train full-time throughout the day, especially if they have to travel to different places to get the entire range of teaching they require. One school may be in the city and another twenty miles away. This dictates constant dedication and understanding, not only from the fighter and his team, but also from any family the fighter has.

It's not easy, by any means.

Add to this schedule the inevitable smorgasbord of personalities that come into play as the fighter assembles his team, and it's easy to see why the life of a professional fighter can be extremely complex and demanding. One coach may want the fighter to work on building up his strength for striking reasons. Another may want him to increase his stretching for pliability on the ground. Still another may want him to focus on roadwork.

It's not that any of the coaches are necessarily wrong, but coordinating the demands they place on the fighter and determining which of the demands takes priority over the others is another task.

For this reason, most fighters have a team of close trusted personal associates—whether it's a manager or even a friend—who they can go to for advice. And sometimes, choosing the person closest to the fighter is the most important decision they make.

Once the team is at last assembled, it's time to start training. This is where the game plan is put under the microscope. Any flaws in the tactics that have been designed to bring victory must be ruthlessly weeded out before fight night.

UFC LEGENDS **Jens "'Lil' Evil" Pulver**

(Photo courtesy Zuffa, LLC)

Fought out of: Davenport, Iowa
Born: 12/6/74
Height: 5'7"
Weight: 155 lbs.
Weightclass: Lightweight
First UFC Lightweight Champion; coach on season five of *The Ultimate Fighter®*

The first man to ever be crowned champion in the UFC at 155 pounds, Jens Pulver survived a harrowing upbringing to become a certified star in mixed martial arts. Known for his "dirty" boxing and concussive power, Pulver's greatest win came on January 11, 2002, when he decisioned heavily favored BJ Penn over five rounds at UFC 35 to retain his lightweight title. The rivalry between the two remains though, and Pulver and Penn met again as coaches and combatants on season five of *The Ultimate Fighter®* reality series.

Sparring

As the fighter trains at his various schools, his individual teachers will be putting him through endless training sessions to improve his skill at new techniques or refine his skill at previously studied tactics. Many of these sessions also will include sparring, but the sparring will generally be limited to the style of the school—for example, ground-fighting sparring will be done at the Jiu-Jitsu school or kickboxing sparring will be done at the Muay Thai academy.

But along with the sparring at each school, the fighter will need a partner that he can try all of his skills out on. Preferably, he will be able to locate a sparring partner somewhat similar to the opponent he will face on fight night. This isn't always possible, but a lot of fighters look to get with someone who is at least somewhat able to give them a taste of what they will be facing.

Time spent training in the ring is time spent refining the game plan. If the sparring partner excels at the same things the opponent does, it will provide immediate valuable feedback to the fighter about how he stacks up. If the fighter thought that elbows and a body slam were going to win him the fight and finds out that they don't work against his sparring partner, then there's a chance they may not work in the Octagon.

Such revelations then demand that the game plan undergo changes that will hopefully put the fighter into a superior position come fight night. And anything that seems out of place or appears that it will not work is usually dropped from the game plan.

As it should be. Fighters have an extraordinary amount on their minds. Game plans must be refined to the point that they are sleek and without too many complications. An easy-to-remember strategy that relies on the fighter's natural skills and gifts is far more likely to work than one that includes every technique and the kitchen sink.

Notable Fights

Ortiz vs. Tanner at UFC 30.

(Photo courtesy Zuffa, LLC)

February 23, 2001: Trump Taj Mahal, Atlantic City, NJ

In the first event since Zuffa LLC purchased the UFC barely a month earlier, UFC 30 was headlined by a power matchup between Tito Ortiz and Evan Tanner. And fans tuned in for some real action.

For Ortiz, the 205-pound championship was on the line. And many regarded his opponent that night as a genuine threat to the crown, as he was an all-around excellent grappler with superb submission skills. Fans and experts alike expected this to be a fierce battle between two imposing and skilled fighters.

Instead, Ortiz ended the match before it really even had a chance to begin. Tanner came out looking to grapple immediately and Ortiz seemed only too willing to give him the chance to close.

Tanner clinched and Ortiz drilled his opponent into the mat with a tremendous slam that knocked the grappler out a mere 30 seconds into round one. Ortiz retained his title and his career continued upward.

Of course, while all of this preparation is going on, the fighter's opponent is across town, across the country, or across the world doing exactly the same thing. And so starts the almost chess match, a battle of strategy and sheer aptitude that will determine the outcome of the fight inside the Octagon.

But even as the fighter has prepared as much as he can with regards to his fighting skills and techniques, there is still a lot to be done before he is ready to step in front of millions of fans on fight night.

The Least You Need to Know

- Fighters and their team examine tapes of previous fights to get insight into their new opponent.

- The team formulates a game plan based on information about the opponent contrasted with the strengths of their fighter.

- The daily schedule of the fighter leading up to fight night is grueling and demanding.

- Sparring is a vital part of fight preparation—preferably using partners that mimic aspects of the upcoming opponent.

Chapter 15

Fine-Tuning the Machine

In This Chapter

- Training for Strength, Speed, and Power
- Agility, Balance, and Flexibility
- Endurance Training
- Nutrition and Weight Management
- Mental Preparation

As the game plan for dealing with the next opponent is being drawn up, and as the fighter is training in various physical techniques, there's an entire aspect that requires the same level of attention: the body of the fighter himself.

All of today's UFC® fighters are first and foremost incredible athletes. It's not easy walking into the Octagon™ as an average man, and few, if any, would recommend doing so. Not when the guy across the Octagon has been training for the fight for months on end. In order to stand toe-to-toe with their opponent, fighters need to be in impeccable condition. And all the conditioning means more hard work.

In this chapter, we take a look at what goes into making an ordinary man a top UFC fighter. We see how they develop strength, increase their speed, and work to deliver powerful shots. We also examine the agility, balance, and flexibility training that helps prepare them to adapt to any situation at a nanosecond's notice. Finally, we take a look at the nutritional side of the equation and finish up with a quick look at the mental game.

Strength, Speed, and Power

No team a fighter puts together is complete without a fitness coach. They are an integral part of the creation of a championship-level fighter. Obviously, if the fighter isn't in good shape, there's simply no hope for a career in the Octagon. So personal fitness trainers, conditioning coaches, or whatever they're called are a vital necessity.

Strength

The physical development of the fighter's body demands that he be strong. One of the easiest ways to go about building strength is through the use of resistance training. This type of training has become extremely popular again for people from all walks of life because it helps build bone strength, muscle strength, and connective tissue strength.

UFC fighters appreciate the idea of building up muscle and bone strength because it means they will be able to hit harder and withstand more punishment than if they did not engage in resistance training at all.

For overall strength, basic weight-training exercises like the bench press, clean and jerk, overhead press, and squats help work the large muscle groups throughout the body. The chest, back, thighs, and arms all benefit from doing sets of these exercises. For more detailed work, weights can be used to target the biceps, triceps, latisimus dorsi, hamstrings, and other smaller muscle groups. The idea is to build up all the muscle groups, but not to the extent that one might see on a professional bodybuilder.

Fighters also focus on the core muscle group, especially with regards to the abdominal muscles. All sorts of exercises, including crunches, twists, sit-ups, leg-ups, and more, help the fighter prepare this important area of his body. The core muscles help the fighter deliver power shots, battle on the ground, maintain his balance, and move fast.

PRO-FILES   **Rising Star: Rashad Evans**

(Photo courtesy Zuffa, LLC)

Fighting out of: Lansing, Michigan
Born: 9/25/79
Height: 5'11"
Weight: 205 lbs.
Weightclass: Light Heavyweight
Light heavyweight contender and winner of the heavyweight division of *The Ultimate Fighter®* season two.

After knocking out Jason Lambert at UFC 63 and Sean Salmon at UFC Fight Night in January of 2007, a lot of people started taking Rashad Evans pretty seriously as a threat to the UFC light heavyweight title. Previously thought to rely strictly on his Division I wrestling background to score wins, Evans showed another dimension to his game when he started knocking people out. Evans, a former hospital security guard who owns a degree in psychology from Michigan State University, trains in Albuquerque and favors the power slam as his favorite technique. One of the UFC's rising stars, it's probably just a matter of time before Evans ascends to the top of the 205-pound division.

Speed

Resistance in another form is used to aid in the development of speed. Many conditioning coaches rely on weight bands, stretchy pieces of rubber that can be adjusted to increase resistance. The springy nature of the bands, along with the tension, help the fighter develop quickness.

Weighted sleds are also popular for fighter training. Strapped into the sled, the fighter must work to pull it a certain distance. The weight on the sled helps build strength and muscle in the fighter's body, while the resistance will help to improve his speed. Once the resistance is gone, the fighter finds himself able to move much faster than before the sled training.

The removal of resistance is the key to developing speed in any and all exercises used by the coaching staff. Fighters work to move fast while tethered to resistance devices. The faster they can go while fighting the resistance, the quicker they will be when that tension is gone.

Power

The development of power relies on both strength and speed to be effective. As a result, power is the natural result of a fighter training to be both strong and quick. The last element that completes the power equation for a fighter would be body alignment.

In this case, let's suppose the fighter is throwing a punch. The punch is the vehicle that will impart power into the target. The muscles of the arm, and indeed the body, propel the fist. The stronger those muscles, the better. At the same time, the fist is moving at a certain rate of speed. The faster that fist flies, the better.

Now we have a strong punch traveling at a certain rate of speed. The last thing a fighter needs is proper alignment to deliver that weapon onto a target. If a fighter's body isn't aimed at the target he wants to hit, there will be a loss of power. If the body is aimed at the target, more power will be imparted upon impact.

Simply stated, if a fighter has his body behind a punch, it will hurt a lot more than if he does not. So to that end, fighters use various training drills to help them develop power.

Coaches will often use focus mitts or pads and move around as the fighter attempts to strike them. By varying the position of the mitts, fighters can work on their ability to aim themselves at targets. When combined with their strength and speed training, these three factors can greatly increase a fighter's power.

Agility, Balance, and Flexibility

Not as glamorous per se as heaving weights around, hauling sleds, or jabbing at focus mitts, exercises that work on agility, balance, and flexibility are nevertheless crucial to overall physical development.

Agility

Fighters need to have quick reflexes in order to adapt to sudden changes in the midst of a fight. Agility enables them to do so, and as a result, many coaches use simple drills to aid in agility training.

Boxers have long relied on skipping rope for developing light footwork. Many mixed martial arts fighters use it as well, but not necessarily to get lighter on their feet. Depending on the fighter, he may not necessarily want to be lighter on his feet, but skipping ropes helps a fighter stay aware and alert, able to move when he wants.

Coaches also might use low hurdles commonly seen on the gridiron during football practice to help their fighters become more agile. The fast pace of hurdles requires fighters to be extremely agile as they run through them.

Plyometric exercises can also help. A plyometic exercise is any movement that causes a muscle to rapidly contract and lengthen immediately followed by another movement that causes the same muscle to rapidly contract and shorten. One particular exercise helps develop both agility and incredibly strong stomp kicks. The fighter squats low first, generating a buildup of power, then comes out of the squat and fires off a front stomp kick. Doing this repeatedly helps build up strength, speed, power, and agility all in one exercise.

UFC LEGENDS   **Matt Hughes**

(Photo courtesy Zuffa, LLC)

Fought out of: Hillsboro, Illinois
Born: 10/13/73
Height: 5'9"
Weight: 170 lbs.
Weightclass: Welterweight
Two-time UFC Welterweight Champion

The premier welterweight fighter of all time, former UFC Welterweight Champion Matt Hughes has dominated the 170-pound weight class for much of his eight-year pro career. A former collegiate All-American wrestler from Eastern Illinois University, Hughes turned to mixed martial arts in 1998 and has never looked back, winning the UFC title in 2001 and 2004, and defending his crown seven times over his two reigns as champion. Among his 42 wins are victories over the elite of the sport, fighters like Royce Gracie, BJ Penn, Georges St-Pierre, Sean Sherk, Frank Trigg, Hayato Sakurai, and Carlos Newton.

Balance

Fighters can work on developing their balance in a number of ways. If they have a more traditional martial arts background, they may wish to practice holding certain postures or stances that will demand good balance.

Fighters also might practice their kicks at a slow rate of speed. Kicking slowly demands a higher degree of control over the body, bringing the leg up and extending it slowly into a target. This has the added benefit of helping develop more speed and strength in smaller muscles.

Depending on the coach, fighters might use something as seemingly strange as a balance beam to help them. Or they may use some of the high-tech gadgets that are sold now, including wobble boards, slalom poles, or even the Swiss ball.

Even without high-tech machines, balance can be worked on easily. Fighters might stand on one foot while tossing and catching a medicine ball with a training partner..

All of these exercises, along with the agility exercises, are designed to help the fighter develop into as well-rounded and capable of a competitor as possible. With fewer weaknesses, a fighter stands a much better shot at winning the bout.

Flexibility

Vital to the physical development of a fighter is the need for flexibility training. Usually, this means that fighters spend some time stretching. While most people are used to seeing fighters stretch during a warm-up, they may not know that stretching is also an excellent way to promote recovery after a grueling workout.

Moreover, stretching helps fighters increase their power in both striking and grappling. Muscles that are stretched and elongated have more blood flowing into them. This helps during a fight by providing vital oxygen and nutrients to the muscles. After the fight, this increased blood flow helps promote faster recovery and healing.

Even a few simple stretches help fighters improve their condition. Sitting down with his legs out in front of him and bending forward to touch his toes is a fantastic all-over body stretch that works muscles running down the back to the hamstrings.

Fighters also might appreciate the relaxing effect that stretching and flexibility training have on them. It's not a bad way to wind down after a long day of training.

Endurance Training

Endurance is one aspect that all fighters need more of. Being able to fight for either three five-minute rounds or five five-minute rounds isn't enough. Fighters need to be able to go on for longer than that if they hope to be able to finish the fight with gas still in the tank.

Endurance training can take a number of forms, and all of them can be grueling. Depending on the fighter, they may only use one or use all of them to help improve their stamina.

Sparring

Previously covered during the development of a fighter's technique, sparring also helps the fighter improve his endurance. Sparring a series of partners over the course of several rounds is a great way to build up stamina. Fighters can see how their techniques change when they start to get tired as opposed to how they fought when they first came out.

Rich Franklin not only fights against several sparring partners, but routinely spars against fighters who have as much as 60 pounds on him. Fighting larger opponents not only increases the challenge to a smaller fighter, but it demands increased awareness, supreme conditioning, and an overall fight ethic that many fighters aspire to.

Roadwork

There is nothing like running to improve lung capacity, endurance, and overall conditioning for a fighter. Running has long been espoused as the single best way to improve stamina, and many coaches still agree. Fighters today might find themselves training out in the mountains where they may run for miles at a time. Urban fighters might take to the city streets, and still other fighters might prefer to use treadmills. It can be done just about anywhere. When training for a fight, most fighters will look to include cardiovascular training at least three times each week in order to build up their stamina.

Swimming

Swimming is another great all-over body method for building up endurance. Some fighters find swimming laps is less punishing to the joints, especially their knees, than roadwork, and many fighters today prefer this method to running. So swimming then becomes their chief source of cardiovascular exercise.

Nutrition and Weight Management

The care and feeding of the body machine is vital for any fighter. Meals become crucial elements of the training process, for both building up and aiding in recovery. Most fighters employ a nutritionist or have studied it enough to be able to create their own diet.

When they're not training for a fight, many fighters will put on weight. This is especially true in the wake of a bout when fighters need to give their bodies plenty of food and rest to speed the recovery process. As a fight approaches, however, fighters will need to drop weight in order to qualify for their division.

Meal Frequency

Fighters don't eat like the majority of ordinary folks. Three meals are simply not enough when they are training full-time. As a result, fighters typically consume at least five meals throughout the day, some as many as seven or eight. Depending on the fighter, the meals may be smaller in terms of volume or not.

Meals are usually consumed either a certain length of time before a workout or in the wake of a workout. Energy drinks and special fluid replenishments also are used to keep the body humming along.

Proteins and Carbs

Fighters will make sure that their meals contain more than enough grams of protein, carbohydrates, and even fats to keep their bodies in peak condition. The usual daily allotments recommended by the government do not apply in this case. Athletes, especially highly trained athletes, need an entirely different nutritional allotment than everyday people.

Proteins—the building blocks of the body—are found in fish, meat, eggs, and dairy products. Carbohydrates—the energy that makes the body go—are found in grains, pasta, and simple sugars like fruit juices.

Supplements

If fighters cannot get enough of the nutrients they need from their meals, they also may use special dietary supplements like protein powders or even multivitamin packs.

Notable Fights

Bonnar vs. Griffin at TUF Finale 1.

(Photo courtesy Zuffa, LLC)

April 9, 2005: Cox Pavilion, Las Vegas, Nevada

In the first season finale of *The Ultimate Fighter®*, fans and UFC officials alike were treated to an awesome display of skill and power as light heavyweight prospects Forrest Griffin and Stephan Bonnar slugged their way through three torrid rounds, earning the respect of all who watched.

With a six-figure contract from the UFC on the line for the winner, Bonnar and Griffin both came out swinging hard. Punches and kicks landed for both men and the tide turned many times throughout the opening stanza.

The second round was more of the same. Griffin swung hard, trying for the home run strike that would earn him the victory. But Bonnar struck right back, landing power shots that would have toppled lesser men. Both fighters went to the ground as well, but they seemed almost evenly matched for the duration.

Round three was a mirror image of the previous two rounds. Bonnar and Griffin, now tired from the battle, kept swinging and proving they had the heart and drive to continue. Again, both fighters landed staggering blows, but they fought it out to the end, forcing the judges to decide the outcome.

In the end Griffin eked out the victory, but in a surprising move, UFC owners also awarded a six-figure contract to Bonnar. The fight remains a fan favorite and clearly illustrates the drive that UFC fighters have to make it all the way to the top.

Even if they are getting what they need from their diets, some fighters elect to use supplements anyway, if only to enhance their diets even further.

Supplements come in powder, liquid, and pill form. Powders are routinely combined with water or juice or even sprinkled onto a meal. Liquids can be self-contained supplement drinks or added to another drink. And pills are swallowed.

Managing the Weight

As the pre-fight weigh-in nears, fighters must take unusually grueling steps to cut the weight they have put on. Stepping on the scales at a weigh-in and not "making the weight" can lead to a cancellation of the fight and the loss of a paycheck, something no fighter wants to have happen.

As a result, fighters are scrupulously alert about tracking exactly what they eat and drink during the pre-fight phase. Each meal is scrutinized for caloric content and the amounts of various nutrients. Fighters calculate how much of everything they are eating to ensure they're getting enough of what they need and also that they will be able to cut the weight without harming themselves.

One of the ways fighters cut their weight is by reducing the amount of food they eat. While they may still eat many meals throughout the day, the number of calories in the meal will be less.

A day or two before the weigh-in, fighters may be desperate to cut weight if they are not where they want to be. They may fast for a day or so, drinking little in the hopes that they can cut "water weight."

If this doesn't work, some fighters may also use a sauna to sweat off water. Dressing in multiple layers that raise their body temperature, fighters will jog or exercise in the sauna, literally sweating off pounds in order to make the weight.

Obviously, this is rather drastic. And fighters must take care that they do not dehydrate themselves too severely; otherwise, they will have a medical emergency on their hands. This is why once they have had the pre-fight weigh-in, most fighters actually put on weight before a fight. They will rehydrate and replenish their stores that have suffered in the quest to drop pounds.

Post-Fight

In the wake of a fight, fighters will immediately eat and rest a great deal. This is vital for their bodies. They have wounds to heal, muscles that need repairing, and in general need to relax for a little while before the next fight. As a result, they will put on weight as their bodies recover and heal.

Before long, however, the next fight is scheduled and the process starts all over again.

Mental Preparation

Along with the physical preparation, all fighters develop some type of mental training. This mental training helps the fighter relax and strategize for the upcoming battle.

Other fighters use meditation to calm themselves and visualize how they will be victorious. Still other fighters use the power of prayer to help them prepare.

Whichever method fighters use to get their "heads on straight," mental preparation is an essential tool to help fighters achieve their goals of becoming championship contenders and victors.

The path to becoming a mixed martial arts fighter is a hard and grueling one. The personal sacrifice, long hours, expense of training, and dedication needed to reach Ultimate Fighting Championship® status is tremendous. But for every fighter, the moment they step into the Octagon, it's all worth it.

For fans, the world of the UFC is adrenaline-packed with fight after fight of superior athletes engaged in sport combat. For the fighters who compete there, the UFC represents the apex of personal achievement, a goal some aspire their entire career to attain.

The roar of the crowd, the thrill of the fight, the glory of victory, and the honor attained stepping into the Octagon—the Ultimate Fighting Championship truly is a sport like no other.

The Least You Need to Know

- Resistance training—with weights or machines—is used to boost a fighter's strength.

- Balance, agility, and flexibility are all just as important to the overall development of a fighter.

- Running, swimming, and sparring are the most common tools used to enhance a fighter's endurance.

- Nutrition and weight management are incredibly important to both preparation for and recovery from a fight.

- Fighters also work on their mental preparation through methods like meditation, visualization, and prayer.

Chapter 16

Born to Fight:
The Rich Franklin Story

When I agreed to help out with this book, I did not realize I would write a chapter myself. Imagine my surprise when the authors sprang the idea on me. I majored in Mathematics in college and argued with most of my professors that classes dependent on essays were unfair to math majors. I was never one for reading many books, and I surely never entertained the idea of writing one. However, in his ultimate treatise, *The Book of Five Rings*, Miyamoto Musashi wrote, "It is said the warrior's is the two-fold Way of pen and sword, and he should have a taste for both Ways."

Rich Franklin.

(Photo courtesy Zuffa, LLC)

My Youth

Born on the south side of the Ohio River, I spent a good portion of my youth growing up in Kentucky. My parents divorced when I was five and I remember a custody battle in which my brother Greg and I spent many hours sitting on benches outside of courthouses.

We moved quite a bit as young children, and I had gone to 13 different schools by the time I graduated high school. Looking back, I wonder how I ever passed the sixth grade after missing over 20 days in the fourth quarter alone. No fault of my own, though, I never was one to miss much school if I didn't have to.

As with most teenagers who have single mothers working 90-hour weeks, trouble began when I finally got a car and my license. I decided to leave my mother's house just before I turned 17 to live with my father.

My dad picked me up on a Tuesday night, and I put a call in to my football coach at Boone County High School Wednesday morning. I explained to him how my living situation had changed, and that I would be coming in later that day to turn in my equipment.

Meanwhile, my dad called Harrison High School's football coach to see if I could start practicing with them. Fortunately they had a spot on the team for me. This was a blessing because most schools had been in two-a-days for a week, and teams were filled. I had to learn a whole new offense, and I was not going to be able to do it by that Saturday, our first scrimmage.

One thing I forgot to mention ... Harrison and Boone County were playing each other that day. It was difficult and embarrassing to shake hands with the opposing team at the end of the game, when I did not even have a chance to explain to most of my friends what had happened. One player looked at me and said, "You were on our team last week!"

First Taste of Martial Arts

Growing up, my life revolved around football and I wanted nothing more than to play professionally. The sad truth is, I didn't even have what it took to be a starter on my high school team, let alone play college or pro. I didn't realize the pro thing wasn't going to work out for me until football season ended my senior year and I didn't have a single college recruiting letter.

Even though football was out, I was determined to maintain an athletic lifestyle of some sort. I walked into a local karate school to check out the class. The instructor, Steve Rafferty, told me it was an advanced class and I needed to come back on beginner night. I told him it wouldn't take me long to be in his class, and I wanted to see what I would be doing in a few weeks. He took a liking to me, and pushed me in my training every day. And that is what I did every day … trained. I trained with him at the school and his house as well. I became good friends with his son, Josh, and Josh and I became longtime training partners.

Shortly thereafter, Steve's other son, Shawn, returned home from his service with the Marine Corps. He began showing us Muay Thai techniques, and I slowly veered from karate classes. All this came about in 1994 after watching several UFC®s. Coincidentally, there happened to be a Gracie Jiu-Jitsu school nearby. I was convinced I needed to begin training on the ground, in case I ever had to actually fight someone. At the time I had no aspirations of fighting professionally.

Unfortunately, not quite two years later Steve's school shut down, and Josh, Shawn, and I were left without a training facility. Shawn and I were attending the University of Cincinnati, and we found some abandoned racquetball courts in Lawrence Hall. We spent a day cleaning them, and months training in them. Several days per week we would meet for sparring and mitt work. I grappled two days per week at the Jiu-Jitsu school, and spent the rest of my time training in Josh's shed.

The backyard shed was no larger than 12 feet by 15 feet. There was no padding on the floor, just a thin layer of used red carpet. I remember grappling when our space heaters only could warm up the shed to 42 degrees.

I had no plans to fight. However, after I attended a local amateur event in Muncie, Indiana, to check out the talent, I told my friends I thought this was something I could excel in. I put 100 percent of my effort into training for my first fight, scheduled for July 1998 in Richmond, Indiana.

Full-Time Fighter

I never really put any thought into the consequence of fighting, which is why I was not concerned about my first fight and didn't even bother warming up. I won handily that night, and that is the primary reason I kept fighting.

Just before that fight I was talking with Kerry Schall about the event. He told me how he was sick and that he was to have been my opponent. I am not sure that would have intimidated me at the time, but I thank God he was sick. Kerry was at least 80 pounds larger than I, because then amateur events disregarded minor details such as weight classes. Since he was from the Cincinnati area, I invited him to train with us at the shed. After seeing our facility, he and his training partner, Steve Martin, thought we were crazy.

At this point, everything began to change direction. I had graduated from college, and started teaching in the fall of 1998. Mark Reitenback bought Excalibur Fitness, the gym where I lifted, and decided to use part of his space as a training facility for fighters. He was not interested in making a profit from that space; we just needed to make sure that portion of the facility maintained itself. I was willing to do just about anything to train in a facility with heat. Josh, Kerry, Steve, and I began training at Excalibur four days a week. We had a 20-foot boxing ring, a 20 × 20 grappling mat, and several hanging heavy bags. We built up a small following of training partners, and the facility was a blessing for the first dozen fights of my career. However, as my professional fighting hobby turned into a career, I quickly began to realize we were outgrowing the facility … not so much in numbers, but in a sense of knowledge and skill.

Management at Last

I met Monte Cox out in Fresno, California, where I was scheduled to fight Aaron Brink in a local promotion. I was so sick for that fight I had to miss the rules meeting two hours before the show began. I was still in my hotel room bed sweating so copiously my fingers looked like prunes. I had a 104-degree temperature, but I did not want to back out of the fight. It was the first time I had been flown to a show, and didn't really know how to handle such a situation with a promoter. Although sluggish and dehydrated, I managed to squeak out a victory.

Several days later, I received a call from Monte asking if Kerry and I would be interested in having him for a manager. Kerry and I took a couple of days to think about it, and decided it was a good idea. Today Monte has so many requests for management we would need to call him. We also took advantage of Monte's affiliation with the Miletich training camp. Kerry, Josh, and I would drive there occasionally to train. It was a perfect way to learn new techniques and gauge us as well. We realized better training partners were a necessity back home. Josh had visited another school on the other side of Cincinnati and told us about the level of training. We all decided to give it a try for one workout.

One workout was all it took to hook me into Jorge Gurgel's school. We had a Brazilian Jiu-Jitsu black belt in the area with dozens of upper-level students. We all began training together as I began my final year of teaching. I was so jealous everyone could train all morning while I had to teach. The following summer was my first experience with full-time training.

Becoming a Full-Time Fighter

Working a full-time job and training at the same time is difficult. I wanted to be working at training rather than working at teaching.

So, even though I had finished my Master's degree in Education and had eight years left on my teacher certification, the decision to quit teaching high school math was not a difficult decision. I knew if fighting didn't work out, I could always return to the classroom.

The first day of summer break for the students was the first day of my new job. Billy Rush had conditioning routines and nutrition programs set up for us. I trained at Jorge's school in the morning with select students, and attended evening classes. I also began branching out to other training facilities. Although we trained MMA at Jorge's school, it was primarily a Jiu-Jitsu school at the time. I had great training partners, but realized I needed coaching if I wanted to fight at the next level. I began to broaden my training base by working with instructors in specific disciplines.

The Impact of Good Coaching

Rob Radford had a boxing gym in a building much like a garage you would use to work on cars. You could smell the sweat that soaked into the canvas in the ring. The lighting was dim, and most of the bags were patched with duct tape. There was a black-and-white mural of Rocky Marciano painted on the wall, and several "Meanest Man" posters. I thought I had found heaven … other than the fact that we dealt with heat issues during the winter, which brought back memories of the shed.

Rob had one boxer in particular I worked with from the first day I was there. James Smith and I sparred every week at the gym and helped each other's learning curve accelerate exponentially. Although I had always considered myself a standup fighter, going to Rob's gym made me quickly realize how little I knew. Jorge and I began driving to Rob's every Wednesday for an hour warm-up with coached sparring and then an hour private. Almost every Wednesday I would leave with a black eye. I am pretty sure it was my technique and not Rob's coaching that earned me a black eye every week.

I began working with Rob a few fights before I worked my way to the UFC. He has had the most impact on my fighting style, and it definitely shows in the Octagon™. I remember him calling me after my first fight in the UFC. He said, "That was an excellent uppercut/hook combo you hit him with." I had no clue what he was talking about, and told him I never threw an uppercut in that fight. It is amazing how your perception of a fight is different from reality when your body is executing trained movements. As I was watching the fight at home I thought, "That was a nice uppercut/hook combo I hit him with."

With all the coaching I received for boxing, I felt as though my kicks were falling behind. I knew I needed to find someone to help me with Muay Thai. We were training at Jorge's school one morning, and by the grace of God, Neal Rowe decided to stop in and check out our training. I believe he wanted to learn ground techniques, but was more than willing to take the time to hold mitts for me. Working with Neal helped me understand how little I knew about Muay Thai. It is a disappointing reality check to realize you are not as good at something as you thought you were. I wanted more focused time with him, and I began traveling to his school for privates.

Neal is famous for his Muay Thai auction … this is where he sounds like he is running an auction, but is actually running me into the ground calling Thai techniques. I began working with him every Monday, and occasionally coming to his school to spar with his students on Tuesdays. Scheduling takes effort when you train at three different facilities. Neal and I had been working together for several months, and I now had a few fights in the UFC. However, I was about to add one more facility to my weekly agenda.

The Quest for Conditioning

Although Billy's position as my conditioning coach was short-lived, he led us to his mentor, Mike Ferguson, and the Powerstation. The Powerstation is the kind of gym most people are intimidated to walk into. If you are worried about carrying a towel with sanitizer to wipe off machines before you use them, you are in the wrong gym. Bars and machines are marred with chalk, and posters of some of bodybuilding's greats are hanging on the wall. Make no mistake, though: this gym is not dirty … just functional. Weights are meticulously placed on the proper racks because Mike's Marine Corp mentality keeps everyone in line. You will rarely hear me say much more than "yes sir" or "no sir" during a workout.

I had all the trainers I needed, and the best in the business at that, but I needed someone looking after my wellness, healing, and recovery from training. I met Dr. David Youtsler at the Powerstation and he invited me to come to his Chiropractic office. He was truly a God-sent blessing … as I found out that full-time training requires recovery time and care as well as training. You could find Jorge and me in his office almost every morning. If we were not getting adjusted, we were taking advantage of the stim, ultrasound and laser machines, which we used for rehabilitating from certain injuries. Doc also takes care of me the week of my fight … making sure I have my vitamins, water, and post-weigh-in meal. He supervises my weight cut, and I usually have to apologize for my moodiness after my fight.

Broken Scales

The scale at the MGM Grand in the men's locker room was broken the day I had to cut weight for my Nate Quarry fight. I had been in the sauna for almost two hours off and on, but the scale told me I had only cut four pounds so far. I still had two pounds to go, and my team and I decided I needed another fifteen-minute session.

I put Doc in charge of the time, and he gave me frequent updates from outside. I put my head down for only a few seconds, but your perception of time in this situation is skewed, and when you are so dehydrated that your mouth does not have enough saliva to break down a piece of gum, time moves even slower.

When I looked through the 12-inch by 12-inch window of the sauna door for a time check, Doc was nowhere to be found. I hollered for him several times, and began to believe everyone had forgotten about me. I was now the only fighter still cutting weight. When Doc returned from his one-minute absence, I began saying things to him I wouldn't want my three-year-old niece to hear. I was sure I had been in the sauna for at least twenty-five minutes, but Doc pressed the stopwatch against the window as it had just passed fourteen minutes.

I am sure he was tempted to leave, but my entire team helped me to cool down. Neal and Rob had towels ready to wrap me in, and Jorge grabbed a few ice cubes. After I was completely dry, I stepped on the scale and my weight was dead on 185 pounds. Two hours later when I stepped on the official scale, I weighed 183 pounds. During fight week, winning my fight is the only thing more rewarding than stepping off the scale after making weight.

Final Thoughts

I think about how complex my weight cut is, and compare that to the simplicity of not even warming up for my first fight. It is a reminder of how complex my life has become during my career as an MMA fighter. I will never forget when Dana White, the president of the UFC, asked me if I was ready to be a "rock star." Beth and I both chuckled at the thought, and could not have imagined how different life would be within the next few months. I often ask myself how one day a person can sign progress reports for students, and another day find himself signing autographs for people waiting in a three-hour line. Life has changed, but despite all of *life's* changes I have tried my best not to let it change *me*.

Glossary of Terms

bridge   A wrestling term. When a fighter on his back and caught in the mount thrusts his hips up and rolls to one side to end up in top position.

butterfly guard   A position utilized by the bottom fighter while ground-fighting that involves being on his back using both ankles to hook inside the thighs of the fighter on top. The knees provide a barrier to keep the top fighter from passing.

centerline   An imaginary line running down the center of the torso and extending beyond into the floor. Controlling an opponent's centerline with footwork enables a fighter to impart more force in his strikes.

choke   A technique whereby the brain is deprived of oxygen and/or blood due to pressure on the carotid artery.

clinch   A position whereby two fighters are in close proximity to one another using grabs to try to control the opponent or set up for a throw or takedown.

combination   A series of strikes, combining punches, elbows, knees, and kicks.

cutman   A specialist in the fighter's corner who treats cuts, bruises, and swelling with the aid of cold metal bars applied with pressure to the wounded area as well as various commission-approved substances.

digging hooks in   After a fighter takes the back of another fighter, he will look to dig his hooks in or position his feet on the inside of the opponent's hips as a means of control.

disqualification   When one fighter is removed from the match for violating the unified rules.

double plum clinch   A position in which both hands are clasped behind an opponent's head with the forearms pressing into the opponent's collarbone area. This position allows for great control in the clinch.

draw   The decision by all three judges that the fight was scored evenly for both fighters. Draws may also occur when one judge votes for each fighter, with the third calling the bout even, or when two judges see the fight even, with the third voting for one of the two fighters.

gap   The space between two fighters.

ground-and-pound   Taking an opponent to the ground and then attacking with strikes to the head and body, whether with punches or elbows.

groundfighting   The process of fighting on the ground.

grappler   A fighter who utilizes pummeling, throws, and takedowns as a means of going to the ground and keeping it there to finish the fight.

guard   While groundfighting, a position the bottom man uses to keep the top man at bay by keeping his legs around the top man's torso and commonly locking the ankles. From this position, the bottom man can sweep, apply a submission, or use limited striking ability.

half guard   During a groundfight, the fighter on bottom has both legs wrapped around one leg of the fighter on top.

headhunter   A fighter who likes to score knockouts using either kicks or punches to the head.

Judo   A Japanese martial art developed by Jigoro Kano emphasizing the use of throws by off-balancing an opponent through positioning. It also uses submissions and pins to gain victory.

Jiu-Jitsu   A term used for martial arts based on the Japanese art of Jujutsu that developed in Brazil. Incorporates groundfighting and submissions.

Jujutsu   An ancient Japanese martial art incorporating all aspects of armed and unarmed combat in its curriculum. Nowadays, Jujutsu usually refers to an art specializing in joint locks, throws, and groundfighting.

knockout   The moment when a fighter renders his opponent unconscious due to strikes.

level change   The process by which one fighter gets his hips lower than the opponent's.

majority decision   When two judges believe fighter A won the bout, but one judge thinks the match was a draw.

mount   The top fighter straddles the bottom fighter around his torso.

Muay Thai   Thai kickboxing art that emphasizes dramatic kicks, knees, elbows, and punches.

Muay Thai clinch   Also the plum clinch, clasping both hands behind the neck of the opponent to deliver knee strikes into the body.

no-contest   When a fighter is injured by an accidental foul before the end of the second round in a three-round fight or before the end of the third round in a five-round fight and cannot continue, then the result would be a no decision.

north-south   During the groundfight, fighters are chest to chest facing the opposite direction.

north-south belly-down   A transitional position that occurs during groundfighting. Exactly the same as a north-south, but both fighters are on their knees.

Octagon™   The arena in which UFC® fighters square off. It is an eight-sided ring roughly 30 feet in diameter.

open guard   When the bottom fighter utilizes the guard, he will commonly unlock his ankles when going for positional change or a submission attempt. Leaving the guard open might allow the top fighter to pass or stand up and back out of the guard position.

overhooks   When a fighter's arms are over the opponent's arms during the clinch.

over-under   A clinch position where both fighters have one arm over and one arm under their opponent.

passing the guard   The process by which the top fighter moves out of the guard into either the half guard or side mount/side control.

pummel   A series of movements in which fighters interlock and exchange hands and arms in an attempt to gain positional control in the clinch.

reversal   Any movement or technique that allows the fighter on the ground to gain topside position or otherwise escape from being on the bottom, also known as the "sweep."

sanctioning   The process whereby a state's athletic commission determines that a sporting event adheres to certain rules and regulations in a professional manner.

shoot   A method by which a fighter ducks low and goes in for a double leg or single leg takedown attempt.

side control   The top fighter lies perpendicular to the fighter on the bottom.

single plum clinch   A position where one hand is behind the opponent's head with the forearm resting on the collarbone while the other hand is free to strike.

split decision   When two judges think fighter A won the bout but one judge thinks fighter B won the bout.

sprawl   A common defense against a double or single leg takedown attempt. It involves shooting out your legs behind you while pressing down on the opponent's head to control his movement.

sprawl-and-brawl   A fight strategy that involves waiting for an opponent to attempt a takedown, sprawling to counter the takedown, and then immediately launching punches, elbows, or knees into the opponent.

stacking   Keeping a fighter on his back and driving his own body weight up and over his neck and head to either escape a submission such as an armbar or to strike.

standup   Any portion of the fight that occurs while both fighters are on their feet.

stoppage   Stopping of the fight at any time by the referee with or without the doctor's advice or the fighter's corner. A stoppage usually results in a TKO for the opponent.

striker   A fighter who predominantly uses punches, elbows, kicks, and knees to win points and fights.

submission   Any type of hold or lock or choke that forces the opponent to tap out or else be placed in further pain, experience a bone break, or temporarily lose consciousness.

technical knockout (TKO)   A method by which a fighter can win; there are two ways to earn a TKO: referee stoppage with or without the doctor's advice, or corner stoppage.

takedown   In wrestling and other groundfighting arts, when a fighter takes an opponent down to the canvas by any of the various types of throws or leg attacks.

taking the back   When one of the fighters is able to basically climb onto the back of the other fighter.

unanimous decision   When all three judges have scored the bout in favor of one fighter.

underhooks   A term for hand position. Double underhooks refer to a fighter having both hands in position under the opponent's arms. Single underhook refers to a fighter who has only one arm under a fighter's arm.

Unified Rules of Mixed Martial Arts   The rules that are used by all Athletic Commissions that have approved the sport of mixed martial arts.

Vale Tudo   The Portuguese term for mixed martial arts competition which literally meaning "anything goes." These competitions utilized fewer rules than today's highly regulated sport.

weight classes   There are five weight divisions in the UFC: lightweight, welterweight, middleweight, light heavyweight, and heavyweight.

MMA Training Centers in the United States

Various Locations

Xtreme Couture
Various locations
http://www.xtremecouture.tv/
Locations.htm

Alabama

BJJ Revolution Team—Samuel Puccio
3020 4th Ave.
Birmingham, Alabama 35233-3008
205-602-2608
samuel@samuelpucciobjj.com
www.samuelpucciobjj.com

Modern Martial Arts Institute
101 First Alabama Bank Dr.
Pelham, Alabama 35124
205-910-4756
Contact: Kevin B. Smith
gurokevin@gmail.com
www.branafightingsystem.com

UMA Jiu-Jitsu
5104 Old Springville Rd.
Clay, Alabama 35126
205-223-3777
Contact: Paul Rhodes
paul@goumakarate.com
www.goumakarate.com

Alaska

Anchorage Brazilian Jiu-Jitsu
3341 Fairbanks St.
Anchorage, Alaska 99503
907-440-0769
Contact: Justin Charon
jcharon@gci.net
www.anchoragebjj.com

Gracie Barra Alaska
401 W. International
Anchorage, Alaska 99518-1104
907-562-0902
www.bjjalaska.com

Arizona

American Martial Arts Center
714 W. Dunlap Rd.
Phoenix, Arizona 85021
602-319-0797
Grapplers@msn.com
www.amacaz.com/

Arizona Combat Sports
1753 E. Broadway
Tempe, Arizona 85282
480-517-1960
azcombatsports@hotmail.com
www.azcombatsports.com

Attitude First Training Center
20633 N. 39th Ave.
Glendale, Arizona 85308
602-370-5781
MMAinfo@attitudefirst.com
www.attitudefirst.com/mma

Roufus Kickboxing Center
1155 W. 23rd St.
Tempe, Arizona 85282-1802
480-966-5425
www.roufuskickboxingcenter.com

Ruffhouse Training Center
20 W. Baseline Rd., Suite #6
Mesa, Arizona 85210
602-434-0197
Contact: Arthur W. Ruff
arthurruff@ruffhousejiujitsu.us
www.ruffhousejiujitsu.us

Warrior Spirit Training Center
515 S. 5th Ave.
Safford, Arizona 85546
928-651-4166
warriorspiritjiujitsu@yahoo.com
warriorspiritjiujitsu.com

West Coast Training Center
1813 E. Baseline Rd., Suite #104
Tempe, Arizona 85283
480-226-8391
Contact: Edwin DeWees
westctc@yahoo.com

Arkansas

Gracie Barra Arkansas
3417 Harrison St.
Batesville, Arkansas 72501
870-612-5000
info@groundfighters.com
www.groundfighters.com

Graveyard Mixed Martial Arts
3417 Harrison St.
Batesville, Arkansas 72530
501-206-5125
info@graveyardmma.com
www.graveyardmma.com

Living Defense Martial Arts
308 E. Kiehl A-4
Sherwood, Arkansas 72120
501-834-3537
Contact: Danny Dring
dannydring@sprintmail.com
livingdefense.com

California

Apex Jiu-Jitsu
25801 Obrero, Suite #11
Mission Viejo, California 92691
949-228-2007
Contact: Jeremy Williams
luvs2knee@yahoo.com
www.apexjiujitsu.com

Apex Jiu-Jitsu—Camp Pendleton
Area 33 Fitness Center
Oceanside, California 92057
949-310-0085
Contact: Rick Estrada or Jason Bukich
apex@subfighter.com
www.apexjiujitsu.com/
CampPendleton/

No Limits Sports & Fitness
16752 Millikan Ave.
Irvine, California 92606
949-251-8822
Contact: Juliano Prado
info@nolimitsfsg.com
www.nolimitsfsg.com

1087 GYM
1087 7th St.
Arcata, California 95521
707-616-2148
1087gym@gmail.com

10th Planet Jiu-Jitsu
7327 Santa Monica Blvd.
West Hollywood, California 90046
Contact: Eddie Bravo
twisterbravo@sbcglobal.net
www.thetwister.tv

American Kickboxing Academy
1830 Hillsdale Ave. #2
San Jose, California 95124
408-371-4235
sal@akakickbox.com
www.akakickbox.com/

Beverly Hills Jiu-Jitsu Club
912 1/2 S. Robertson
Los Angeles, California 90035
310-854-7664
Contact: Marcus Vinicius
mvbhjjc@aol.com
www.bhjjc.com/

Boran Jiu-Jitsu
1548 Adams Ave., Suite #D
Costa Mesa, California 92626-3816
714-751-7505
Contact: James Boran
avalanchenyc@sbcglobal.net
www.boranjj.com

Brazilian Jiu-Jitsu Club
11650 Riverside Dr. #5
Studio City, California 91602
1-877-548-4877
Contact: Chris Lisciandro
jiujitsuclub@sbcglobal.net
www.brazilianjiujitsuclub.com

Brazilian Top Team Long Beach
1335 Loma Ave.
Long Beach, California 90804
562-331-0138
Contact: Marcelo Perdomo
MarceloPerdomo@hotmail.com
braziliantopteamlongbeach.com

Bruddas
9223 Folsom Blvd.
Sacramento, California 95826
916-369-2384
charlesgracie.com/academy-sacramento.htm

Caique Jiu-Jitsu Academy
19751 S. Figueroa St.
Carson, California 90745
310-618-8149
besafe@caiquejiujitsu.com
www.caiquejiujitsu.com/

Callide Jiu Jitsu
5643 Cahuenga Ave.
Burbank, California 91505
818-762-0097
www.callide.com

Carley Gracie Jiu-Jitsu Academy
30 Seventh St., Third Floor
San Francisco, California 94103
415-788-0454
academy@gracie.com
www.carleygracie.com/

Centerline Gym
9812 Belmont St.
Bellflower, California 90706
562-208-1771
Contact: Jerry Wetzel
breakunose1@aol.com
www.centerlinegym.com

Charles Gracie Academy
309 8th Ave.
San Mateo, California 94401
650-756-7579
charles@charlesgracie.com
www.charlesgracie.com

Chute Box
19069 Beach Blvd.
Huntington Beach, California 92648-2305
310-272-3831
Contact: Roberto Piccinini
http://www.chuteboxe-usa.com/contact.php

Cleber Luciano Brazilian Jiu-Jitsu
6070 Warner Ave.
Huntington Beach, California 92647
714-842-4554
cleberjiujitsu@verizon.net
www.cleberjiujitsu.com

DeLaO Brazilian Jiu-Jitsu
8381 Katella Unit E
Stanton, California 90680
714-527-1845
Contact: John Delao
john.delao@delaojiujitsu.com
www.delaojiujitsu.com

Fabio Santos Brazilian Jiu-Jitsu
4780-F Mission Gorge Place
San Diego, California 92120
619-229-0022
fabio@fabiojiujitsu.com
www.fabiojiujitsu.com

Fairtex Muay Thai & Fitness
132-140 Hawthorne St.
San Francisco, California 94107
415-777-5888
Contact: Anthony Lin
anthony@fairtexmuaythai.com
www.fairtexmuaythai.com

Fight and Fitness
734 Bryant St.
San Francisco, California 94107
415-495-2211
Chris@FightandFitness.com
www.fightandfitness.com/

Fight Science—Abrigo Martial Arts
3935 Sepulveda Blvd.
Culver City, California 90230
310-927-4045
burnlaugh@yahoo.com
www.abrigomartialarts.com

Global Brazilian Jiu-Jitsu
1725 D3 Monrovia Ave.
Costa Mesa, California
949-645-8060
webmaster@globalbjj.com
www.globaljiujitsu.com

Gokor Chivichyan
5123 Sunset Blvd., #214
Los Angeles, California 90027
323-660-5202
gokor@gokor.com
www.gokor.com

Gracie Barra Lake Forest
22661 Lambert St., #209
Lake Forest, California 92630
949-951-4796
Contact: Marcio Feitosa
feitosagb@yahoo.com.br
www.graciebarrausa.com/

Gracie Jiu-Jitsu Academy
1951 W. Carson St.
Torrance, California 90501
310-782-1309
info@gracieacademy.com
www.gracieacademy.com

HITS Training Academy
7044 Sunrise Blvd., Suite #A4
Citrus Heights, California 95610
916-284-0087
J_Harris@hotmail.com
www.hitstraining.com

Hollywood BJJ
1106 N. La Cienega Blvd., #103
West Hollywood, California 90069
310-360-0544
shawn@hollywoodbjj.com
www.hollywoodbjj.com/

House of Discipline
902 Cardiff St.
San Diego, California 92114
619-697-6475
luisdl@hodtkd.com
www.hodtkd.com

Integrated Martial Sciences
1220 Soquel
Santa Cruz, California 95062
831-566-4672
Contact: Brian Burns
contact@ims-pankration.com
www.ims-pankration.com

International Kickboxing & Combative Arts
16165 Brookhurst St.
Fountain Valley, California 92708
714-775-0200
Contact: Jerry Huffman
info@ikickbox.com
www.ikickbox.com

Jean Jaques Machado BJJ
18750 Oxnard St., #403
Tarzana, California 91356
818-343-6548
jjm@jeanjacquesmachado.com
www.jeanjacquesmachado.com

Krav Maga Training Center
11500 Olympic Blvd.
West Los Angeles, California 90211
310-966-1300
michaelm@kravmaga.com
www.kravmaga.com

LA Boxing Costa Mesa
600 Anton Blvd., 11th Floor
Costa Mesa, California 92626
1-866-LABOXING
Contact: Sean McCully
www.laboxing.com

Leka Vieira BJJ Academy
1618 Gramercy Avenue
Torrance, California 90501
310-320-8520
leka1@sbcglobal.net
www.lekavieira.com/

Lion Training Center
1217 Glenoaks Blvd.
Glendale, California 91201
818-549-9933
www.liontc.com/

Lister Training Center
1020 Tierra Del Rey, Suite #D
Chula Vista, California 91910
619-920-6719
www.listertrainingcenter.com

Millennia Jiu-Jitsu
9375 Archibald Ave., Suite #802
Rancho Cucamonga, California 91730
909-989-9044
Contact: Romie Aram
romiea@millenniajiujitsu.com
www.millenniajiujitsu.com

Oakland Karate & Kickboxing
3300 Broadway
Oakland, California 94611
510-444-7616
Contact: John Morrison
J_Morrison@oaklandkarateandkick-boxing.com
www.oaklandkarateandkickboxing.com

OC Muay Thai
3079 South Harbor
Santa Ana, California 92704
949-228-8833
Contact: David
info@OCMuayThai.com
www.ocmuaythai.com

Open Door Brazilian Jiu-Jitsu
2935 Chapman St.
Oakland, California 94601
415-724-4088
sergiogralha@yahoo.com
www.opendoorbjj.com

Orange County Kickboxing
18241 McDurmott West, Suite #B
Irvine, California 92614
949-833-9833
www.ockickboxing.com

PB Fight Center
4878 Cass St.
San Diego, California 92109
858-273-1344
www.rodrigomedeirosbjj.com

Progressive Martial Arts
1320 Calle Avanzado
San Clemente, California 92673
949-498-9489
Contact: Bryon Schnell
progressivema@cox.net
www.progressivemartialarts.net

R1 Training Center
113 Sierra St.
El Segundo, California 90245
310-322-5552
webmaster@r1gym.com
www.r1gym.com/

Ralph Gracie Jiu-Jitsu—San Francisco
178 Valencia St.
San Francisco, California
415-552-4777
www.ralphgracie.com/

Ralph Gracie Jiu-Jitsu Orange County
1150 Yorba Linda Blvd.
Placentia, California 92870
714-524-7880
Contact: Brad Jackson
rob@ralphgracie.com
www.ralphgracie.com/

Rex Muay Thai Kickboxing
14661 Lanark St.
Van Nuys, California 91402
818-786-7922
muaythai2004@sbcglobal.net
www.rexmuaythai.com/

Rey Diogo BJJ
8733 Venice Blvd.
Los Angeles, California 90034
310-839-9086
reydiogo@yahoo.com
www.reydiogo.com/

Rickson Gracie International Jiu-Jitsu
11755 Wilshire Blvd., Suite #40
West Los Angeles, California 90025
310-914-4122
rgjjcenter@rickson.com
www.rickson.com/

Rigan Machado BJJ
977 E. Colorado Blvd.
Pasadena, California 91106
626-792-5050
info@riganmachado.com
riganmachado.com

Rodrigo Clark Brazilian Jiu-Jitsu
121 E. Mason St., #A
Santa Barbara, California 93101
805-259-9720
Contact: Rodrigo Clark
rodrigoclark@rodrigoclark.com
www.rodrigoclark.com

Roy Harris Academy
8250 Camino Santa Fe, Suite #J
San Diego, California 92121
royharris@runbox.com
www.royharris.com/

Russian Combat Sambo Training Center
1035 W. MacArthur Blvd.
Emeryville, California 94608
415-246-1239
Contact: Val Pashchenko
valpashchenko@gmail.com
www.ruscombatsambo.com

Showtime Brazilian Jiu-Jitsu
819 E. La Habra Blvd.
La Habra, California 90631-5531
562-691-0333
www.showtimejiujitsu.com/

SLO Kickboxing
956 Foothill Blvd., Unit #B
San Luis Obispo, California 93401
805-549-8800
info@slokickboxing.com
www.slokickboxing.com

Solution Fitness
1955 Lucile Ave.
Stockton, California 95209
209-688-1412
Contact: Justin Pfeifer
www.solutionfitness.com

South Bay Jiu-Jitsu
325 Pacific Coast Highway
Hermosa Beach, California 90254
310-318-8960
Contact: Bob Bass
bobbass@southbayjj.com
www.southbayjj.com/

Street Sports
3011 Ocean Park Blvd.
Los Angeles, California 90405
1-877-jiu-jitsu
Contact: Renato Magno
streetsportsjj@hotmail.com
www.streetsportsbjj.com

Team Magnitude Brazilian Jiu-Jitsu
1910 Shadowridge Dr., Suite #107
Vista, California 92081
760-291-9585
Contact: Michio Grubbs
teammagnitude@cox.net
www.teammagnitude.com

The Boxing Club Kearny Mesa
4164 Convoy St.
San Diego, California 92111
1-800-BOXING-CLUB
www.theboxingclub.net

The Boxing Zone
1351 Palm Ave.
Imperial Beach, California 91932
619-429-UBOX (8269)
info@theboxingzone.com
www.theboxingzone.com

Tinguinha BJJ Academy
1035 N. Armando St., Suite #K
Anaheim, California 92806
714-630-6218
www.tinguinha.com

Todd Medina's Freestyle Fight School
140-B E. 17th St.
Costa Mesa, California 92627
949-646-6224
info@fightschool.com
www.fightschool.com

U.S. Blackbelt Academy
30251-C Golden Lantern
Laguna Niguel, California 92677
949-363-6500
Contact: Ivan Kravitz
usba@sbcglobal.net
www.usblackbeltacademy.com

Ultimate Fitness
1705 I Street
Sacramento, California 95814
916-444-3357
http://ultimatefitness.pro/

Ultimate Kickboxing & Fitness
414 Tennessee St., Suite #I
Redlands, California 92373
909-792-7844
Contact: Robert
robert@ultimatekick.com
www.ultimatekick.com

United Fighting Systems
9637 Arrow Rte., Building 4, Suite #C
Rancho Cucamonga, California 91786
909-919-0775
Contact: Jeff Frater
jefffrater@ufs.kungfusansoo.info
ufs.kungfusansoo.info

USA Storm
1105 El Vecino Ave.
Modesto, California 92656-6212
209-527-6033
lance@usastorm.com
usastorm.com

Wander Braga Glendale BJJ
1217 W. Glenoaks Blvd.
Glendale, California 91201-2201
818-549-9933
wander@wanderbraga.com
www.wanderbraga.com

World Muay Thai Gym
26516 Ruether Ave., Unit #207
Santa Clarita, California 91350
661-251-3840
www.worldmuaythaigym.us

Colorado

Brazilian Jiu-Jitsu Boulder
1750 30th St., Unit #22
Boulder, Colorado 80303
303-938-1275
www.bjjboulder.com

GRAPPLER'S EDGE Submission Fighting
5305 E. Colfax Ave.
Denver, Colorado 80220
303-433-EDGE (3343)
info@grapplers-edge.com
www.grapplers-edge.com

High Altitude Martial Arts
12200 E. Cornell Ave., Suite #P
Aurora, Colorado 80014
720-404-7744
Contact: Nate
valetudo7@hotmail.com
highaltitudema.com

Stars Training Center
#8 Garden Center
Broomfield, Colorado 80020
303-410-1824
pancrase@starzworld.com
www.starzworld.com

Connecticut

Royce Gracie Jiu-Jitsu Network of Norwich
433 W. Main St.
Norwich, Connecticut 06360
860-889-1818
charliepkarate@yahoo.com
www.gracienorwich.com

Southern New England MMA
161 Woodford Ave.
Plainville, Connecticut 06062
860-989-1419
Contact: John
info@snemma.com
www.snemma.com

Ultimate MMA
33 State St.
North Haven, Connecticut 06473
203-668-6110
Contact: Andrew Calandrelli
tapuoutct@yahoo.com

Florida

ATT Headquarter Gym
4631 Johnson Rd., Suite #1
Coconut Creek, Florida 33073
954-425-0705
Contact: Ricardo Liborio
info@americantopteam.com
www.americantopteam.com

Body Dynamics
900 Pasadena Ave. S.
South Pasadena, Florida 33707
727-321-9875
Contact: Shane Dunn
bodydjen@hotmail.com
www.bodyd.com

Brazilian Jiu-Jitsu Center
1594 E. Commercial Blvd.
Ft. Lauderdale, Florida 33334
954-771-0084
Contact: Pablo Popovitch
info@bjjcenter.com
www.bjjcenter.com

Chi Martial Arts
9699 N.E. 2nd Ave.
Miami Shores, Florida 33138
305-759-6565
Contact: Aaron Fruitstone
chimartialarts@bellsouth.net
www.chimartialarts.com

Extreme Martial Arts
12605 S.W. 134th Court
Miami, Florida 33186
305-439-7421
Contact: Michael Cardoso
info@extrememma.com
www.extrememma.com

Freestyle Fighting Academy
1423 S.W. 107th Ave.
Miami, Florida 33174
305-225-4610
Contact: Marcos Avellan
MarcosFFA@bellsouth.net
www.floridamartialarts.com

Freestyle Fighting Academy
1423 S.W. 107 Ave.
Miami, Florida 33176
305-225-4610
Contact: David Avellan
freestylefight@bellsouth.net
www.freestylefighting.net

Gracie Barra Orlando
2906 Corrine Dr.
Orlando, Florida 32803
407-228-1160
jiujitsuclub@bellsouth.net
marciosimas.com

Gracie Barra Tampa
7235 W. Hillsborough Ave.
Tampa, Florida 33654
727-204-9731
veio@eduardodelima.com
www.tampabjj.com/

Gracie Miami School of Self Defense
3165 N.E. 163rd St.
North Miami Beach, Florida 33160
305-354-2060
Contact: Pedro Valente
pedro@graciemiami.com
schoolofselfdefense.com

GriffonRawl
Hillsborough/Hanley
Tampa, Florida 33610-4147
352-544-1197
Contact: Dan Rawlings
muay_thai@griffonrawl.com
www.griffonrawl.com

Lotus Club
Florida—Conde Jiu-Jitsu Team
8419 W. Macnab Rd.
Tamarac, Florida 33321
754-264-9270
Contact: Luiz Felipe Amarante
lotusclub@condejiujitsuteam.com
www.condejiujitsuteam.com

One Dragon Martial Arts
9101 Taft St.
Pembroke Pines, Florida 33024
954-443-4183
info@onedragon.com
www.onedragon.com

Tallahassee Mixed Martial Arts Club
1416 West Tennessee St.
Tallahassee, Florida 32304
850-556-0941
Contact: Harrison Pfeiffer
grappler_x@hotmail.com

Team Popovitch Brazilian Jiu-Jitsu
1594 E. Commercial Blvd.
Ft. Lauderdale, Florida 33334
954-771-0084
Contact: Fred Moncaio
info@bjjcenter.com
www.bjjcenter.com

Georgia

Alliance Jiu-Jitsu Atlanta
10 Krog St.
Atlanta, Georgia 30307
404-843-0606
Contact: Romero "Jacaré" Cavalcanti
info@alliancebjj.com
www.alliancebjj.com

Creighton Mixed Martial Arts
3775 Peachtree Crest Dr.
Duluth, Georgia 30097
770-331-1794
Contact: Paul Creighton
jiujitsu33@hotmail.com
www.paulcreighton.com

Ground Zero Fighting Systems
4487 Columbia Rd.
Augusta, Georgia 30809
706-877-3279
Contact: John Oliverio
augustafighter@yahoo.com
www.groundzerofighting.com

Knuckle Up MMA/Fitness
5956 Roswell Rd.
Atlanta, Georgia 30342
404-943-0609
www.knuckleupmma.com/

Hawaii

Brazilian Freestyle Jiu-Jitsu
Athletic Complex, Studio #2,
University of Hawaii at Manoa
Campus
Manoa, Hawaii
808-223-9363
Contact: James Tanaka
info@brazilian-freestyle.com
www.brazilian-freestyle.com

Idaho

Alliance Jiu-Jitsu Boise
2201 E. Park Center Blvd.
Boise, Idaho 83706
208-345-4653
Contact: Mitch Coats
mcoats911@msn.com

Golds Gym Training Center
801 E. Park Center Blvd.
Boise, Idaho 83702
208-345-4563
Contact: Nate Pettite

Kosen Jiu-Jitsu Academy
4347 Jordyn # A
Pocatello, Idaho 83202
208-406-7574
Contact: Mark Massey
judolawdog@yahoo.com
www.judokanjiujitsu.tripod.com

Primal Tribe Fighting
Eagle Call For Directions
Boise, Idaho 83704
208-631-0488
Contact: Tom Supnet
jango@cableone.net
www.primaltribefighting.com

Illinois

Curran Martial Arts
2D Crystal Lake Plaza
Crystal Lake, Illinois 60014
815-356-0454
Contact: Chuck Pilcher
cpilcher@teamcurran.com
www.teamcurran.com

Hackney's Combat Academy
800 W. Lake Street, Suite #108
Roselle, Illinois 60172
630-351-1209
hackneyscombat.com

Nikko-Ki Training Club
4910 Hydraulic Rd.
Rockford, Illinois 61108
815-509-7687
Contact: Frank
nikkoki1@aol.com
nikko-ki.com

Peoria Athletic Club
1221 S.W. Adams St.
Peoria, Illinois 61602
309-672-3090
Contact: Coach Ryan
blackrby@mtco.com
www.peoriaathleticclub.com

Indiana

Carlson Gracie Jiu-Jitsu—Team Wally
2437 Miracle Ln.
Mishawaka, Indiana 46545
574-220-8727
Contact: Wally
wally@carlsongracieteam.com
www.carlsongracieteam.com

Integrated Fighting Academy
24 S. Shelby Street
Indianapolis, Indiana
317-345-1316
www.ringsports.net

Kentucky

Four Seasons Martial Arts Gym
1591 Winchester Rd., Village East
Shopping Center
Lexington, Kentucky 40505
859-245-5082
mma4s@yahoo.com
www.4smma.com

Miletich Fighting Systems of Kentucky
5623 Taylor Mill Rd.
Taylor Mill, Kentucky 41015
859-393-9590
Contact: Scott O'Brien
obrienmfs@hotmail.com
mfs-kentucky.tripod.com

Louisiana

Lake Area BJJ
1440 Nelson Rd.
Lake Charles, Louisiana 70601
337-540-6900
Contact: Mike Ellender
info@labjj.com
www.labjj.com

Maine

Academy of Mixed Martial Arts
468 Forest Ave.
Portland, Maine 04102
201-712-5955
Contact: Jay Jack
ammaonline.com

Maryland

Baltimore Martial Arts
8450 Baltimore National Pike
Ellicott City, Maryland 21043
410-465-7799
Contact: Gary Berger
info@baltimoremartialarts.com
www.baltimoremartialarts.com/

Lloyd Irvin Martial Arts Academy
6333 Old Branch Ave., Suite #302
Camp Springs, Maryland 20748
301-449-kick
Contact: Lloyd Irvin
info@lloydirvin.com
www.lloydirvin.com

Ryoma Academy
10500 New Georges Creek Rd.
Frostburg, Maryland 21532
301-689-9856
Contact: Kevin Wilson
www.evolveacademy.com

Sekai Martial Arts
2420 Churchville Rd. Unit #3
Churchville, Maryland 21015
410-734-9545
Contact: Ronald, Lenny
info@sekaimartialarts.com
www.sekaimartialarts.com

Xtreme MMA
9540 Holiday Manor Rd.
Perry Hall, Maryland 21236
443-629-9860
Contact: Haki K.S. Lee
admin@xtrememma.net
www.xtrememma.net

Yamasaki Academy
5609 Fishers Ln., Suite #6A-7A
Rockville, Maryland 20852
301-770-0969
Contact: Mario Yamasaki
info@grappling.com
www.grappling.com

Massachusetts

Best Way Jiu-Jitsu
27 Rockland St.
Rockland, Massachusetts 02370
774-274-6250
dedeco@bestwayjiujitsu.com.br
www.bestwayjiujitsu.com

Boston Brazilian Jiu-Jitsu
10 Dedham St.
Newton, Massachusetts: 02461
Phone: 617-969-9901
www.bbjiujitsu.com

Brazilian Martial Arts Center
700 Mystic Ave., 2nd Floor
Somerville, Massachusetts 02145
617-628-3800
Contact: Marcelo Siqueira
bmacboston@hotmail.com
www.brazilianmartialartscenter.com/

**Chinese Kickboxing and
Submission Fighting Club**
4293 Washington St.
Roslindale, Massachusetts 02131
617-469-8233
Contact: Paul Rosado
info@chinesekickboxing.com
www.chinesekickboxing.com

Franklin Martial Arts
16 E. Central St.
Franklin, Massachusetts 02038
508-553-2888
www.franklintkd

Harvard Judo Club
MAC Recreation Room 1
Harvard University
Cambridge, Massachusetts 02138
Contact: Club President
Judo@hcs.harvard.edu
www.hcs.harvard.edu/~judo/

Massachusetts Submission Academy
45 High St.
Clinton, Massachusetts 01510
978-365-6197
Contact: Keith Rockel
masssubacademy@aol.com
www.masssubmissionacademy.com

Massachusetts Brazilian Jiu-Jitsu
2 School St.
Acton, Massachusetts 01720
978-795-3300
Contact: Patrik Barbieri
info@massbjj.com
www.massbjj.com

Massachusetts Submission Academy II
47 Sumner St.
Milford, Massachusetts 01757
508-254-1096
Contact: Matt Phinney
mattphinneyjj@hotmail.com

MIT Judo Club
Dupont Athletic Center
Cambridge, Massachusetts 02139
Contact: Club President
judo-request@mit.edu
web.mit.edu/judo/

Northeastern University Judo Team
Marino Center Studio B
Northeastern University
Boston, Massachusetts 02115
Contact: Rick Bertucci
www.judo.neu.edu/Information/ContactUs

Pedro's Judo Center
19 New Salem St.
Wakefield, Massachusetts 01880-1905
781-245-0644
Contact: Jimmy Pedro
info@pedrosmartialarts.com
www.pedrosmartialarts.com

Silver Dragon Progressive Martial Arts
439 Main St.
Indian Orchard, Massachusetts 01151-1238
413-543-8877
Contact: Keith or Chris
silverdragon371@aol.com
www.silverdragonpma.com

Sityodtong U.S.A.
100 Broadway
Somerville, Massachusetts 02145
617-625-9678
Contact: Mark Dellagrotte
usabranch@sidyodtong.com
www.sidyodtong.com

Tohoku Judo Club
444 Somerville Ave.
Somerville, Massachusetts 02144
617-776-9060
Contact: Vittorio Recupero
judoka@earthlink.net
TeamTohoku@aol.com
home.earthlink.net/~judoka/

United States Mixed Martial Arts
316 Hartford Ave.
Bellingham, Massachusetts 02019
508-966-5006
Contact: Jorge Rivera
tom@usmma.org
www.usmma.org

Michigan

Burke's Wrestling Academy
8803 Hall Rd.
Utica, Michigan 48317
586-354-6468
Contact: John Burke
abwrestlingclub@comcast.net
www.eteamz.active.com/
burkewrestlingacademy

Minnesota

Minnesota Martial Arts Academy
6840 Shingle Creek Parkway, Suite
#24
Brooklyn Center, Minnesota 55430
763-560-5696
info@mmaacombatzone.com
www.mmaacombatzone.com

Warrior's Cove
3004 Texas Ave., #S
St. Louis Park, Minnesota 55426
952-935-0140
Contact: David Arnebeck
info@warriorscove.com
www.warriorscove.com

Missouri

Absolute Martial Arts
3221 S. Kingshighway
St. Louis, Missouri 63139
314-664-0466
Info@Absolute-Martial-Arts.Com
www.absolute-martial-arts.com

Blue Springs Jujitsu
5225 W. 40 Highway, Building #6
Blue Springs, Missouri 64015
816-224-2822
Contact: Wayne Marble
www.myjujitsuschool.com

Trinity Martial Arts
16650 E. 40 Highway
Independence, Missouri 64055
816-804-8146
Contact: Randy Blair
randalblair@juno.com
www.trinitymartialarts.org

Ultimate Martial Arts, LLC
201 N.W. 11th St.
Blue Springs, Missouri 64015
816-878-5586
Contact: Kirby Minor
info@ultimatemartialarts.tv
www.ultimatemartialarts.tv

Vaghi Martial Arts
177 Concord Plaza
St. Louis, Missouri 63128
314-842-8850
www.submissionjiujitsu.com

Montana

Dogpound Submission Fighting
2501 S. Reserve St.
Missoula, Montana 59801
406-370-3928
www.dogpoundfighting.com

Nevada

Cobra Kai Jiu-Jitsu
2104 Highland Ave.
Las Vegas, Nevada 89102-4622
702-395-4567
Contact: Marc Laimon
marclaimon.com/

Las Vegas Combat Club
3655 S. Durango
Las Vegas, Nevada 89147
702-791-5822
Contact: Jeff Mulhollan
jeff@lvcombatclub.com
www.lvcombatclub.com

Xyience Training Center
3655 South Durango, Suites 5-6
Las Vegas, Nevada 89147
702-838-8008
http://www.xyiencetrainingcenter.
com/error.php

New Jersey

Advanced Fighting Systems
262 Franklin Turnpike
Mahwah, New Jersey 07430
201-828-5860
www.thaing.net

**America's Finest Karate/
Kickboxing and BJJ Academy**
607 Westfield Ave.
Elizabeth, New Jersey 07208
908-354-1014
Contact: Jonas Nunez
info@afkka.com
www.afkka.com

Basulto Academy of Defense
7707 Bergenline Ave.
North Bergen, New Jersey 07047
201-692-0746
Contact: Armando Basulto
info@wayofnoway.com
www.wayofnoway.com

Bergen County Boxing
111 Spring St.
Ramsey, New Jersey 07446-1151
Phone: 201-236-9510
Contact: Lou Coticchio
lou.coticchio@bcboxing.com
www.bcboxing.com

Camal Judo
86 Lackawanna Rd.
West Paterson, New Jersey 07424
973-632-4933
Contact: Anthony Camal
info@camaljudo.com
www.camaljudo.com/contact.htm

Cornerstone Martial Arts
10 N. 26th St.
Kenilworth, New Jersey 07031
908-906-4322
Contact: James Meals
cornerstonemartialarts@hotmail.com
www.cornerstonemartialarts.net

Cranford Judo & Karate Center
107 South Ave. W
Cranford, New Jersey 07016
908-276-3544
Contact: Yoshisada Yonezuka
www.cranfordjkc.com

Dover Boxing Club
10 Tierney Rd.
Lake Hopatcong, New Jersey 07849
973-663-0500
Contact: Ed Leahy
blucky17@optonline.net
www.doverboxingclub.com

Endgame Combat Sports Academy
1 Dell Glen Ave.
Lodi, New Jersey 08644
973-478-1324
www.teamendgame.com

Gladiator Boxing
699 Challenger Way, Unit #5
Forked River, New Jersey 08731
609-971-3668
Contact: Shawn Darling
Gladiatorboxing@comcast.net
www.boxinggyms.com/gladiator.htm

Guerrero Brazilian Jiu-Jitsu/MMA Academy
201 Bloomfield Ave., Suite #6
Verona, New Jersey 07044
973-239-3866
Contact: Rigo
kneeonbelly@msn.com
www.kneeonbelly.com

Hassett Jiu Jitsu
422 Delsea Dr.
Sewell, New Jersey 08080
856-218-8333
www.hassettskarate.com

Infinite Martial Sports
112 S. Washington Ave.
Bergenfield, New Jersey 07621
201-387-1811
Contact: Ace Ramirez
www.imsports.net

Jerry Jones Ultimate Martial Arts
45 Franklin Ave.
Nutley, New Jersey 07110
973-662-9662
www.jjultimate.com

Jersey Mixed Martial Arts Academy
1432 Rte. 70 East
Cherry Hill, New Jersey 08034
215-467-1008
Contact: Brad Daddis
braddaddis@comcast.net
www.jerseymma.com

Kokushi Dojo
11 Madison Ave.
Westwood, New Jersey 07675-1721
Phone: 201-573-0026
www.kokushi.com

M B S Martial Arts Academy
428 Tenafly Rd.
Tenafly, New Jersey 07670
201-894-0014

Montclair Brazilian Jiu-Jitsu Academy
356 Bloomfield Ave., #2
Montclair, New Jersey 07042-3625
973-454-0352
Contact: Mike Mrkulic
www.mbjj.com

Nisei Kito Ryu Jiu-Jitsu
3153 Fire Rd.
Egg Harbor Township, New Jersey 08234
609-383-9801
Contact: Sergio DeCasien
sdecasien@aol.com
www.freewebs.com/nkjj/

North Jersey Judo
574 Newark Pompton Turnpike
Pompton Plains, New Jersey 07444
201-206-2705
Contact: Ramon Hernandez
ramon@northjerseyjudo.com
www.northjerseyjudo.com

North Jersey Muay Thai
95 B Dell Glen Ave.
Lodi, New Jersey 07644
973-835-8577
Contact: Joe Bumanlag
www.northjerseymuaythai.com

Performance Brazilian Jiu-Jitsu Academy
24-08 Broadway/Rte. 4 East
Fairlawn, New Jersey 07410
201-225-0000
Contact: Louis Vintaloro
www.armlock.com

Planet Jiu-Jitsu
460 Ridgedale Ave.
East Hanover, New Jersey 07936
973-493-0557
Contact: Jeff Miller
planetjj@optonline.net
www.martialartsnj.com

Professional Karate Academy
65 Chestnut St.
Red Bank, New Jersey
732-842-8597
Contact: David M. Lentz
info@professionalkarate.com
www.professionalkarate.com

Real Martial Arts and Fitness
1750 Brielle Ave., Unit #A6
Ocean, New Jersey 07712
732-695-9555
Contact: Sensei Brian Wright
info@realfightingdojo.com
www.realfightingdojo.com

RGDA BJJ
1288 Van Houten Ave.
Clifton, New Jersey 07013
973-851-4772
Contact: Efrain Rojas
err27@yahoo.com
www.erbjj.com

Savarese Martial Arts Academy
482 Stuyvesant Ave.
Lyndhurst, New Jersey 07071
201-368-2865
Contact: Chris Savarese
savbo@optonline.net
www.njbjj.com

Shadow Boxing Academy
74 South Ave.
Fanwood, New Jersey 07023
908-322-1744
Contact: Mr. Knight
info@shadowboxingacademy.net
www.shadowboxingacademy.net

Shore Thing Wrestling Club
175 Oberlin Ave.
Lakewood, New Jersey 08701-4566
732-295-9047
Contact: Vin
psstwc@aol.com
www.shorething.homestead.com/
index.html

South Mountain Martial Arts
91 Main St.
Madison, New Jersey 07940
973-822-1977
Contact: Dayn DeRose
daynd@aol.com
www.smma.net

Spartan School of Self Defense
112 Palisade Ave.
Cliffside Park, New Jersey 07010-
1037
201-943-0090
www.spartandojo.com

Tech Judo Club
2136 85th St.
North Bergen, New Jersey 07047
201-869-6600 ext. 2518
Contact: Leonardo Victoria
clydeapajudo@aol.com
www.techjudo.com

The EDGE Ultimate Martial Arts
7 Midland Ave.
Elmwood Park, New Jersey 07407
201-703-1222
www.edgekickboxing.com

Tri-State Brazilian Jiu-Jitsu Academy
85-99 Hazel Street
Paterson, New Jersey
973-842-2605
Contact: Edson Carvalho
carvalhoteam@yahoo.com
www.edsoncarvalho

Vizzio's Ringside Fitness
600 Secaucus Rd.
Secaucus, New Jersey 07094
201-223-kick
Contact: Vizzio
info@vizzio.com
info@vizzio.com

New Mexico

FIT NHB
110 Lomas Blvd. N.E.
Albuqeurque, New Mexico 87104
505-833-3351
Contact: Tom & Arlene Vaughn
FITNHB@aol.com
fitnhb.com

Jackson's Mixed Martial Arts
5505 Acoma S.E.
Albuquerque, New Mexico 87110
Phone: 505-881-7911
jacksons.tv/

New York

Bellmore Kickboxing Academy
2551 Merrick Rd.
Bellmore, New York 11710
516-679-5997
Contact: Chris Cardona
info@bellmorekickboxingacademy.
com
www.bellmorekickboxingacademy.com

Borodin's Gym
2209 Avenue Z
Brooklyn, New York 11235
718-332-7993
Contact: Vladimir Borodin
muaythainy@aol.com
www.borodinsgym.com

Church Street Boxing Gym
25 Park Place
New York, New York 10007
212-571-1333
Contact: Boxing Instructor
info@churchstreetboxing.com
www.nyboxinggym.com

Combined Martial Arts Academy
34-05 Steinway St.
New York, New York 11101
718-389-9494
Contact: Steven Katz
stevenkatz@rhinofightteam.com
www.combinedmartialarts.com

D'Arce BJJ
1570 Brentwood Road
Bay Shore, New York 11706
631-968-6208
Contact: Joe D'Arce
joedrc@optonline.net
www.darcejiujitsu.com

Defend University of New York
53 Kensico Rd.
Thornwood, New York 10594
914-747-5707
Contact: Steve Kardian
info@nydefendu.com
www.nydefendu.com

East Coast BJJ Academy
320 Yonkers Ave.
Yonkers, New York 10701
Contact: Sean Alvarez
tasbjj@hotmail

Elite Defensive Tactics
Rt. 202
Yorktown, New York 10598
914-962-3267
Contact: Larry Byrnes
EliteDefensiveTactics.com
EliteDefensiveTactics.com

Empire Judo
605 Culver Rd.
Rochester, New York 14623
585-943-1652
Contact: Chris Chzog
EmpireInfo@Bushin.org
teamempire.us

Empire Martial Arts
1892 Central Ave.
Colonie, New York 12205-4200
518-456-2582
Contact: Alan Condon
www.empirekarate.com/

Evolution Combat Club
5650 Merrick Rd.
Massapequa, New York 11758
516-826-8970
evomma@optonline.net
www.evolutioncombatclub.com

Fabio Clemente Brazilian Jiu-Jitsu Academy
98 3rd Ave., 2nd floor
New York, New York 10003
212-529-7675
Contact: Fabio Clemente
clementefabio@hotmail.com
www.newyorkjj.com

Fighthouse
122 W. 27th St., 2nd floor
New York, New York 10001
212-807-9202
Contact: Multiple instructors
info@fighthouse.com
www.fighthouse.com

Gleason's Gym
83 Front St.
New York, New York 11201
718-797-2872
Contact: Bruce Silverglade
info@gleasonsgym.net
www.gleasonsgym.net

Hudson Valley Jiu-Jitsu
1222 Hopewell Ave.
Fishkill, New York 12524
845-255-3318
Contact: Brian Mclaughlin
brian@bjjfighter.com
www.bjjfighter.com/hvjj/

International Martial Arts Academy
601 W. Jericho Turnpike
Huntington, New York 11743
631-385-2312
Contact: Ray Longo
ray@raylongomartialarts.com
raylongomartialarts.com/index.html

Jason Morris Judo Center
575 Swaggertown Rd.
Scotia, New York 12302
518-399-3936
Contact: Jason Morris
silver92@albany.net
www.realjudo.net

Kingsway Boxing Enterprises
1 W. 28th St., 2nd floor
New York, New York 10010
212-679-3427
Contact: Michael Olajide
info@kingswaygym.com
www.kingswaygym.com

Kioto BJJ
200 Wilson St.
Port Jefferson, New York 11776
631-331-0100
Contact: Master Mansur
admin@kiotobjjny.com
www.kiotobjjny.com

Lotus Club NY
25-14 34th Ave.
New York, New York 11106
646-594-4371
Contact: Eduardo Santos
bjjlotusnyc@gmail.com

Louis Neglia Martial Arts Academy
365 Avenue U
Brooklyn, New York 11223
718-372-9089
Contact: Louis Neglia
lou@louneglia.com
www.louneglia.com

New York Combat Sambo
15 W. 39th St., 4th floor
New York, New York 10018
718-728-8054
Contact: Stephen Koepfer
americansamboassociation@att.net
www.nycombatsambo.com

NY Sanda
336 W. 37th St.
New York, New York 10018
212-239-8619
Contact: David Ross
ikfmdc@att.net
www.nysanda.com

Oishi Judo Club
79 Leonard St.
New York, New York 10013
212-966-6850
Contact: Sensei Oishi
oishijudo@att.net
www.oishi-judo.com

Relson Gracie Jiu-Jitsu New York Academy
26 Columbus Ave.
Tuckahoe, New York 10707
646-228-1945
Contact: Mike Casey
info@gracieny.com
www.gracieny.com

Renzo Gracie Academy
224 W. 30th St., Suite #0100
Manhattan, New York 10001
212-279-6724
info@renzogracie.com
www.renzogracie.com

Ronin Athletics
122 W. 27th St.
New York, New York 10001
Phone: info@roninathletics.com
Contact: Christian Montes
www.roninathletics.com

Serra Jiu-Jitsu East Meadow Academy
2554 Hempstead Turnpike
East Meadow, New York 11554
Phone: 516-520-2052
www.serrajitsu.com

Serra Jiu-Jitsu Huntington Academy
601 W. Jericho Turnpike
Huntington, New York 11743
Phone: 631-385-2312
Contact: Matt Serra
www.serrajitsu.com

Sitan Gym
25-73 Steinway St.
Queens, New York 11103
Phone: 718-932-5000
kickboxing@sitangym.com
www.sitangymny.com

Soca Brazilian Jiu-Jitsu
2508 Merrick Rd.
Bellmore, New York 11710
Phone: 516-785-5000
Contact: Soca
soca@socabjj.com
www.socabjj.com

Starrett Judo
1310 Pennsylvania Ave.
New York, New York 11239
Phone: 718-240-4530
Contact: Parnel Legros
info@starrettjudo.org
www.starrettjudo.org

Staten Island Judo Jujitsu Dojo
12 Jefferson Blvd.
New York, New York 10314
Phone: 718-984-4600
Contact: Nick Fulciniti
info@sijjd.com
www.sijjd.com

The Blitz Center
28-30 W. 36th St.
New York, New York 11103
212-244-8500
Contact: Marcos Santos
sportjiujitsu@yahoo.com
www.blitzcenter.com

Tiger Schulmann's
39 W. 19th St.
New York, New York 10011
1-800-52-TIGER
www.TSK.com

Ultimate Sambo Academy
133 N. Main St.
Florida, New York 10921
845-651-5155
Contact: Mrs. Koulikov
ykoulikov@optonline.net
www.ultimatesambo.com

Wat
31 Howard Street
New York, New York 10013
212-966-4010
Info@TheWat.com
Contact: Ed Kalkay (media contact)
http://www.thewat.com/enter.html

World Oyama Karate Academy
203 Main St.
White Plains, New York 10601
914-681-0640
Contact: Sensei Sakai
sakai@oyamakarate-njny.com
www.oyamakarate-njny.com/index.htm

North Carolina

Alliance Jiu-Jitsu of Charlotte
1607-G Montford Dr.
Charlotte, North Carolina 28209
704-477-8552
Contact: Luis "Sucuri" Togno
sucuri@sucuribjj.com
www.sucuribjj.com

New Bern Jiu-Jitsu
3000 Hwy 70 West
Havelock, North Carolina 28560
252-617-2566
Contact: Jerry Moreno

TEAM ROC
6829 Fillyaw Rd., Suite #102
Fayetteville, North Carolina 28303
919-906-2640
Contact: Spenser Canup
amma@teamroc.net
www.teamroc.net/

Ohio

Pedro Sauer BJJ at Summit Martial Arts
425 S. Sandusky St.
Delaware, Ohio 43015
740-362-2222
Contact: Charles Riedmiller
riedmiller1@cs.com
www.summitmartialarts.com

Relson Gracie BJJ
6831 Flaggs Center Dr.
Westerville, Ohio 43081
614-890-2340
Contact: Robin Geisler
robin_gieseler@yahoo.com
www.gracieohio.com

Oklahoma

Academy of Martial Arts
1110-5 South Air Depot
Midwest City, Oklahoma 73110
405-205-2895
Contact: Kentric Coleman

Titan Martial Arts
1628 W. Lindsey
Norman, Oklahoma 73069
405-306-3751
Contact: Justin Mullinax
justin@titanmartialarts.com
www.titanmartialarts.com

Oregon

Straight Blast Gym
12945 S.W. Beaverdam Rd.
Beaverton, Oregon 97005-2126
503-350-3926
oberhue@straightblastgym.com
www.straightblastgym.net

Team Quest Training Center
18206 S.E. Stark St.
Portland, Oregon 97233
503-661-4134
Contact: Robert Follis
robert@tqfc.com
www.tqfc.com

Pennsylvania

Body Arts Gym
926 N. 2nd St.
Philadelphia, Pennsylvania 19123
215-520-9682
Contact: Angel Cartagena
info@bodyartsgym.com
www.bodyartsgym.com

Bucks County Kickboxing & Mixed Martial Arts
3613 Old Easton Rd.
Doylestown, Pennsylvania 18901
949-244-5567
Contact: Eric Karner
erickarner@worldmma.com
www.worldmma.com

Bucks County Kickboxing & Mixed Martial Arts
21 W. Butler Ave.
Chalfont, Pennsylvania 18914
215-822-0848
Contact: Eric Karner
erickarner@worldmma.com
www.worldmma.com

Ephrata Martial Arts
248 W. Fulton St.
Ephrata, Pennsylvania 17522
717-738-2244
Contact: Sifu Justin Press
ephratamartialarts@hotmail.com
www.ephratamartialarts.com

Mark Shrader's Mixed Martial Arts Academy
60 W. Peters St.
Uniontown, Pennsylvania 15401
724-439-4545
Contact: Mark Shrader, Belinda Hoone
markskarate@yahoo.com
www.marksmma.com

Philadelphia Mixed Martial Arts Academy
1321 S. Juniper St.
Philadelphia, Pennsylvania 19147
215-467-1008
Contact: Brad Daddis
braddaddis@msn.com
www.phillymma.com

SteelCity Martial Arts
3561 Valley Dr.
Pittsburgh, Pennsylvania 15234
412-835-5544
Contact: Sonny Achilles
Steelcityma@aol.com
www.steelcitymartialarts.com

Rhode Island

Battleground Training Center
461 Main St.
East Greenwich, Rhode Island 02818
401-886-9229
Contact: Chris
chriscwj@yahoo.com
www.battlegroundtrainingcenter.net

South Carolina

Alliance Jiu-Jitsu of Greenville
1322 E. Washington St., Suite #C-1
Greenville, South Carolina 29601
864-420-1646
Contact: Billy Fletcher
www.alliancegreenville.com

Columbia Self-Defense
1315-A Gadsen St.
Columbia, South Carolina 29201
803-799-9455
Contact: Jack Walker/Matt Fulmer

South Dakota

Action MMA
4200 W. 42nd St.
Sioux Falls, South Dakota 57106
605-321-6105
Contact: Bruce Hoyer
bruce@dakotagrappling.com
www.actionmma.com

Tennessee

Guardian MMA
1720 Old Fort Parkway
Murfreesboro, Tennessee 37129
615-895-1667
Contact: Cliff Fonseca
guardianjiujitsu@bellsouth.net
www.guardianjiujitsu.com/index.htm

Individual Fighting Systems
709 Little Brook Rd #2
Cookeville, Tennessee 38501
615-866-4201
Contact: Andrew Kodger
ifsinc@gmail.com

Kapellers Taekwondo
2374 Cedar St.
McKenzie, Tennessee 38201
731-352-0700
Contact: Arthue Kapeller
kapellersfamilytaekwondo@hotmail.com
lisasroadtozion.tripod.com/
kapellersfamilytaekwondo/

Memphis Judo & Jiu-Jitsu
3472 Plaza Ave. #101
Memphis, Tennessee 38111
901-355-8091
Contact: David Ferguson
fdavidbjj@aol.com
www.memphisbjj.com

Texas

Ashcrafts Martial Fitness
4522 Fredricksberg Rd., #A-49
San Antonio, Texas 78201
210-736-4272
Contact: Chip Thornsburg
chip@ashcrafts.net
www.ashcrafts.com

Baker's Martial Arts
1711 W. Beauregard
San Angelo, Texas 76901
325-656-2396
Contact: Troy Baker
martialarts@mindspring.com

Bushi Ban
7770 Spencer Highway
Pasadena, Texas, 77505
281-479-7979
webmaster@bushiban.net
www.bushiban.net/

Carlos Machado BJJ
13720 Midway Rd., Suite #210
Dallas, Texas 75244
972-934-1316
jiu-jitsu@sbcglobal.net
www.carlosmachado.net

Definitive Martial Arts
5211 A Kleinbrook
Houston, Texas 77066
281-701-5901
Contact: Travis Tooke
ttooke22@yahoo.com
www.travistooke.com

Denton BJJ
3261 N. Elm St. (US-77)
Denton, Texas 76207
469-549-9919
Contact: Kirk Gibson
contactus@teamgibson.net
www.teamgibson.net

Force Academy
800 County Rd.
Burkburnett, Texas 76354
940-636-1597
Contact: Preston Campbell
forcefighting@yahoo.com

Force Academy
105 North Ave. D
Burkburnett, Texas 76354
940-636-1597
Contact: Preston Campbell
forcefightingsystems@yahoo.com

Houston BJJ Club
11902 Jones Rd.
Houston, Texas 77070
281-770-3670
Contact: Art
www.hbjjc.com

Infinite Jiu-Jitsu
254 W. Fm 1626
Buda, Texas 78610
512-694-6095
Contact: Darrin Lillian
Darrin@InfiniteJJ.com
www.infinitejj.com

Infinite Jiu-Jitsu
2110 West Slaughter Lane, Suite 165
Austin, Texas 78748
512-282-1444
Contact: Darrin Lillian
Darrin@infinitejj.com
www.infinitejj.com

Krav Maga-Performance Fitness & Self Defense
1328 McDermott
Allen, Texas 75013
469-939-1949
Contact: Eric
performanceselfdefense.com
www.performanceselfdefense.com

North Dallas Mixed Martial Arts
700 W. Spring Creek
Plano, Texas 75023
972-679-4387
modernwarrior@comcast.net
www.ndbjj.com

Paragon Brazilian Jiu-Jitsu
6313 Wooldridge, Suite #8
Corpus Christi, Texas 78414
361-549-3597
www.ccparagonbjj.com

Saekson Janjiria Muay Thai
3033 W. Parker Rd., #202
Plano, Texas 75023
972-769-8663
saekson@saekson.com
www.saekson.com

TABMOC
77 Heaven Blvd.
San Antonio, Texas 78258
555-210-7777
www.tabmoc.com

Vasquez Academy
5736 Manchaca Rd., #370
Austin, Texas 78745
512-891-0880
vasquezacademy@netzero.com
www.vasquezacademy.net/

Utah

Pedro Sauer Brazilian Jiu-Jitsu
9460 S. 560 West
Sandy, Utah 84070
801-561-2535
www.pedrosauer.com

Rigan Machado BJJ of UTAH
1629 N. State St.
Orem, Utah 84057
801-434-9316
Contact: Mickey
wonchoitkd@hanmail.net
wonchoitkd.com

Virginia

Capital Jiu-Jitsu Academy
305 Hooff's Run Dr.
Alexandria, Virginia 22314
703-346-8828
Contact: Jeremy LaFreniere
jeremy@gracieva.com
www.gracieva.com

Gustavo Machado
2696 Reliance Dr.
Virginia Beach, Virginia 23452
757-749-9814
Contact: Gustavo Machado
gustavojjmachado@hotmail.com
www.gustavomachado.com

Hybrid Martial Arts Center
4323 Williamson Rd.
Roanoke, Virginia 24012
540-345-8609
Contact: Dennis Hayes
pancadinha@aol.com
www.hybridfighting.homestead.com

Jiu-Jitsu Now Academy
20099 Ashbrook Place
Ashburn, Virginia 20147
703-955-9034
Contact: Andrew Correa
andrew@jiujitsunow.com
www.jiujitsunow.com

Krav Works
132 W. Jefferson St.
Falls Church, Virginia 22046
703-533-3993
Contact: Asher Willner
KravWorks@gmail.com
www.capitalkravmaga.com

Modern American Mixed Martial Arts
Middle Ground
Newport News, Virginia 23602
757-236-2546 or 757-342-3600
Contact: Giovanni Lemm or Nick White
mammasboymma@yahoo.com
www.geocities.com/mammasboymma

Team Lloyd Irvin Martial Arts
3801 Wilson Blvd.
Arlington, Virginia 22203
703-807-0342
www.novamma.com

Winchester Brazilian Jiu-Jitsu
304 S. Loudoun St.
Winchester, Virginia 22601
540-662-3057
Contact: George Wehby
winbjj@yahoo.com
www.freewebs.com/winbjj

Washington

Lotus Club Auburn
4210 Auburn Way N. Site 5
Auburn, Washington 98002
253-208-3270
Contact: Lotus Club Auburn
coach@lotusclubjiujitsu.com
www.lotusclubjiujitsu.com/washingtonaub.htm

Ring Sports United
1900 132nd Ave. N.E., #A-6
Bellevue, Washington 98005
425-576-5300
Contact: Mark Messer
www.ringsportsunited.com/index.htm

US Judo Training Center
355 Rainier Ave. N
Renton, Washington 98055
425-226-1655
www.judochampions.com

West Virginia

Academy of Mixed Martial Arts
SIU Box 809
Salem, West Virginia 26426
304-782-1372
Termi1@aol.com
www.fighting-tigers.com/amma

Advanced Boxing Kickboxing & Jiu-Jitsu
800 Campbells Creek Dr.
Charleston, West Virginia 25306
304-549-9370
AdvancedBKJ@yahoo.com
www.advancedbkj.com

Ground Zero Jorge Gurgel
914 1/2 4th Ave.
Huntington, West Virginia 25701
304-522-7088
ashleymlockwood@hotmail.com
www.gzfs.8m.com

Wisconsin

Badgerland Jiu-Jitsu Center
4104 Milwaukee St.
Madison, Wisconsin 53714
608-438-6275
Contact: Mark Severtson
webmaster@badgerlandjiujitsu.com
www.badgerlandjiujitsu.com

Duke Roufus Gym
111 West Virginia St.
Milwaukee, Wisconsin 53204-1641
414-319-1151
dukeroufusgym@sbcglobal.net
www.dukeroufusgym.com

Fox Valley Grappling Club
2605 W. College Ave.
Appleton, Wisconsin 54914-4202
920-450-3172
foxvalleygrapplingclub@yahoo.com
www.foxvalleygrapplingclub.com

Henry Matamoros Jiu-Jitsu
2653 S. Kinnickinnic Ave.
Milwaukee, Wisconsin 53207
414-431-1888
webmaster@henrymatamoros.com
www.henrymatamoros.com

Madison Jiu-Jitsu Academy
2038 E. Washington Ave.
Madison, Wisconsin 53704-5206
608-279-4154
Contact: Mark Plavcan
madisonbjj@grapplermail.com
madisonbjj.homestead.com

Third Heaven Martial Arts
114 Front St.
Beaver Dam, Wisconsin 53916-2102
877-342-8708
www.thirdheaven.com

Index

G